Find more of my work at my blog:

www.theauthorstack.com

Find all my work at my website:

www.russellnohelty.com

Bookbub:

https://www.bookbub.com/profile/russell-nohelty

HOW TO THRIVE AS A WRITER IN A CAPITALIST DYSTOPIA

By:
Russell Nohelty

Edited by:
Lily Luchesi

Proofread by:
Toni Cox

First Edition, February 2025

MY THESIS ABOUT HOW TO THRIVE AS A WRITER IN A CAPITALIST DYSTOPIA

I will be the first to admit that this is not a scholarly text. While I did learn from hundreds of sources to compile it, this book is more a manifesto than anything. I've been doing this work for over 20 years, and almost every problem writers complain about is rooted not in any one platform but in the structural constraints of capitalism as a whole.

That does not mean I'm wholly against capitalism. I think capitalism is dumb and evil but consistent and gameable. I don't need something to be logical to be useful, and that is the main crux of the argument in this book. You won't find a treatise on burning down capitalism because I don't think we can burn it down. I think we can extricate ourselves from the evils of capitalism and enlighten others as to the ills of capitalism, but this text is filled with tactical and practical advice on how to exist within the economic system and burn it down from the inside.

Mostly, I want writers to stop burning out, and even though I've written three other books on author growth, none of them deal with the underlying systemic bullshit that comes with capitalism. This book is different. It dives deep into the structural issues of capitalism on writers, how it holds us back, and how we can live inside it without selling our souls.

Before we start talking about how you, as a creative type, can thrive in the capitalist dystopia we find ourselves currently trapped inside, I thought you might like to know the thesis of my argument for why writers struggle so much when they go about building a sustainable creative business.

- Writer think all this creative business stuff works *logically* and/or *intuitively.*
- When they start doing it though, they quickly find that none of this stuff works the way they think it should work.
- When it doesn't work how they think it will, creatives get anxious/depressed/frustrated/angry, causing them to spiral and quit.

This leads to a lot of pain and aggravation. Good news, though.

- While it is not intuitive, capitalism does work consistently, even if not logically. While writers expect A to equal B, A actually equals Xylophone. However, it does so (more or less) consistently.
- If you understand how this stuff works consistently and can replicate it, then you will start having success.
- If you start having success, you will get more confident.
- If you are more confident, then you will keep doing making cool things.
- If you keep making things, I get to consume more weird, cool stuff.

The job of this book is to show you how to make A consistently equal Xylophone in a way that works sustainably for you.

The universe is dumb, and capitalism is nonsense, but at least it is consistent nonsense, which makes it gameable and thus winnable. Once you know how to translate it properly, the whole world starts to makes a whole lot more sense, even if only in the nonsensical way that *Alice in Wonderland* follows an internal logic.

Finally, this will not be a political hit piece. Capitalism affects people across the political spectrum in the same way. It is the base operating system for every facet of our lives and this book is simply meant to help you learn how to exist better within it in a way that works for you.

That, in a nutshell, is what we're talking about here. This book attempts to parse what capitalism is and isn't, how to extricate yourself from the parts that don't work for artistic pursuits, and how to embrace the underlying bits that can work for our businesses and build something beautiful from it.

Ready? Then, let's get started.

THE UNIVERSE IS DUMB, AND CAPITALISM IS NONSENSE

Do you ever find yourself saying, "I understand this is how it works, but it's so dumb?"

I find myself doing this all the time. My wife and I often turn to each other and say, "I get it, but it's dumb."

We had a dishwasher repairman talk to us about how new dishwashers are way worse than they used to be, even as they get more energy efficient. He told us how to keep ours from stinking like it has since we got it.

When he left, I said, "I get it, but it's dumb."

When I teach people how to succeed at this work, I often tell them, "It is dumb that the world works this way, but putting that aside, it is how it works, even though it makes no sense".

In fact, I am starting to think that many people fail to succeed because they can't rationalize how dumb it all is and how stupid most of the things that work really are when you get down to it.

Even the things that make sense are usually pretty dumb. The same is true with entrepreneurship. If I'm not saying how dumb something is, then I'm wondering why everything is so hard all the time.

I've been thinking a lot about why building a creative writing business is so hard. So today, let's talk about five reasons why it's so hard to do this work.

THE MARGINS ARE LOW, AND THE COMPETITION IS HIGH

If you look at the overall entrepreneurial space, the low-end products tend to be pocket courses or monthly memberships ranging from $27 to $47.

Then, on top of that, people sell courses or other products that range from $99 to $999+.

Most businesses make their living selling these higher-end products and use the lower-end products to pay for ad spend.

Meanwhile, a writer generally either has a membership for $5 to $10/mo or a book for $5 to $40, depending on the format.

So, the high-end offer a writer offers is not even as expensive as the low-end offer most businesses use to generate interest in their higher-end offers.

My Writer MBA business partner, Monica Leonelle, calls this The Novelist's Dilemma. Even if you have 50 books, you can probably only charge at most $250 to $500 for an ebook collection of what must have been years or decades of your work.

Meanwhile, I could, and have, recorded a course in 2 days and charged $1000 for it. I can make more selling one course than I do from over 100 ebook sales.

Fiction authors can't do the same type of thing, which puts them at a structural disadvantage.

Additionally, the competition for books is astronomically high, driving down pricing.

This is the opposite of the popular Blue Ocean Strategy, which is the ability of a business to find new markets without much competition. Within, people look for business opportunities where there is no competition. It's about making high-priced, unique offers in areas where nobody else fights for the same audience.

Books, and writing in general, is a red ocean. It is filled with millions of people vying for the same pool of readers. There are unlimited books right now and not unlimited humans to read them.

No books could ever be written again, and we would have enough knowledge to last us a hundred years.

Every year, we add more information than we did for the first several thousand years of written history combined.

So, when you're thinking about why this is so hard...it's because this is really hard. Like, very, very, very hard. It's harder than most businesses out there.

You have chosen to play the game in hard mode by doing this work, and your frustration is, frankly, warranted.

In fact, I always tell people that if publishing didn't exist and I went into business school to ask if I should start a company where the margins are low, the profits are low, the competition is fierce, and there's a race to the bottom in pricing, everyone would tell me no.

And yet, we persevere.

This is the secret advantage here because, in general, most people fall away. There is so little money in publishing that most entrepreneurs run away for greener opportunities.

There is not enough money opportunity to stick around for the long haul. Publishing is, at best, a weigh station for most people.

However, it gives people who stick around a real advantage because it shows they are cut from the same kind of crazy to want to do this work, and simply by doing it for long enough, you set yourself apart.

All the institutional knowledge you gain becomes your advantage as others abandon it for new opportunities.

It's not a great silver lining, but it is one that doesn't exist in many other industries.

THERE ARE NO PAIN POINTS

Almost all successful businesses sell on a pain point. Whether it's, "lose 30 lbs in 30 days", "get out of debt", or "save money by shopping here", or something else, they can pull out a pain point to convince people to act. Selling fiction is hard because there is no clearly defined pain point besides, "I want a new book, and you have one."

Instead, we have to form a bond with our audience on a deeper level to connect their need to belong and feel seen with our work.

I call this "soul resonance selling", which is about finding people who resonate with the same frequency of weirdness as you, and it's much harder than pain point selling.

Imagine a book vibrating with the same frequency as your body, and simply touching it sends a jolt through you. That's what I'm talking about with soul resonance selling.

We must bake that resonance deep into our work so it calls out to the right people.

There are many people I don't like, but I listen to them because they are geniuses at solving certain problems.

I do not follow any fiction writers, memoirists, or creative non-fiction writers I don't resonate with because why would I?

There are infinite books out there, and I don't need yours…except I do need to feel seen, and soul resonance selling is about showing people they are seen in a deep and meaningful way.

This creates more loyal fans of your work but is also a higher-order need.

Love and belonging sit above physiological needs and safety and security in Maslow's Hierarchy of Needs, and the minute one of those other needs presents itself, the need to belong becomes secondary or tertiary.

In the same way, "nice-to-haves" are the first to be cut in a recession, people will put their safety and security above their need to belong when the bills come due.

It's very easy to say, "Well, I love their work, but I have to eat," with creative writing because there is no clearly defined pain point.

However, in every household, there are a couple of pleasures that people take, even in the worst of times. I contend that the need to belong and feel seen is the most important in the darkest days.

We must, then, try to find ways to deepen the connection with the reader so that even in the dark of the night, they still feel most seen when they read our work.

If we can do that, we can still become an integral part of their lived experience and have a chance to stay a part of their lives in those dark times and make things a little better for them.

We must be the singular subject matter experts they rely on even when they turn everything else off. We must create the series they reread every year because it speaks to them on a primal level.

We can do this by turning more deeply into our universal fantasies, our shared language, and our subject matter expertise. We must dig deeper if we want to build those deeper connections.

And we must do them before the bad times come because, in the darkness, we usually don't have the energy to make those new connections.

The deeper we can forge those connections, the more people will resonate with our message and the deeper they will resonate.

If we can get really good at soul resonance selling, it makes everything else much easier.

However, it also means thinking about sales in a different way. It means being more empathetic and giving much more than you ask.

For instance, if somebody emails me they are struggling, I will always send them some of my books to help them through a tough time.

Often, I get emails from people in hospice care, and I'll give them access to everything I do, even though I get zero benefit from it except connecting with a human in their darkest hour.

It's these things where we live our truth that help deepen that connection even more.

You see, selling isn't really about sales. It's about how we craft things with care and move through the world.

If we can do that, then when we launch something people will want to support it, and it won't feel like sales at all.

THE POWER LAW CURVE IS RUTHLESS

If you are the 10th best (or 100th best, depending on size) plumber in your city, you are probably making a decent living. If you're the 50th best accountant in your area, you probably have a good job.

Yes, the absolute best accountants are doing better than you, probably even significantly better than you, but you can still make a decent living, even if you are in the middle of the curve.

That's not true in creative businesses, which have the most brutal power law curve of any other industry. For our purposes, I'm talking about how the authors at the top make exponentially more than the people at the bottom or even in the middle. You can think of this as the Pareto Principle, where 20% of your actions lead to 80% of your results, but on steroids.

Most people understand the Pareto principle, but did you know that it repeats within itself?

Inside that initial 20% that drives 80% of the outcomes, for instance, just 20% of those actions result in 80% of those results, which repeats again from there.

When I work with authors, I often tell them that while they are doing a good job on the surface-level Pareto Principle, they need to dig deeper to find the 20% of those actions driving growth and continue drilling down until they find the true core of their business.

But let's get back to the power law curve. You see this curve everywhere in every industry, especially with investing.

However, in creative industries, the power law curve is the most skewed I have ever seen.

The people at the top of the curve don't just make exponentially more than those in the middle…they make ALL the money.

90% of the money in writing is earned by only 10% of the authors, and do you want to guess how that distribution goes when you dig in deeper?

If you guessed that 90% of that income is distributed to 10% of that original 10%, you would be just about right.

The global book market was recently estimated to be worth around $90 billion, meaning that $81 billion was distributed to the top 10% of authors, leaving $9 billion for the remaining 90% of authors.

That's pretty brutal, but there is a supercharged version of the Pareto Principle at work here as well.

This means that of that $81 billion, roughly $72 billion was distributed to the top 1% of people, leaving $19 billion to be distributed to 99% of authors.

It sounds like a lot, but Wal-Mart made $611 billion last year by itself.

This is why you're likely not seeing monetary gains even as your audience grows. ***It's not a function of you not being good enough.***

It's that ***all*** the cards are stacked against you, even if you've been doing this a long time.

Getting into the top 10% of the publishing industry is relatively easy, but there's not a ton of money at that level. You must go above the 90th percentile to see significant monetary gains.

If you're in the top 10% of any other industry, you're killing it financially, but not in creative industries.

The power law curve works against you when it comes to growth, too.

If you're in the top 10%, you're in the 90th percentile of earners. If you want to grow beyond that, you have to expend as much energy to get from the 90th percentile to the 91st percentile as you did to get from 1st to the 90th percentile, and the energy expenditure gets harder from there.

You then have to spend as much energy to get from the 91st to the 92nd percentile as you did to get from the 1st to the 91st percentile, and it keeps going on like that until you reach the top.

The energy is not arithmetic; it's exponential and becomes harder with each percentage gained.

Why?

Because the people at the top are staying there and are committed to not losing relevance. To rise, you must wedge your way inside between increasingly smaller and smaller gaps.

It becomes much more relational at the upper end of the power law curve. At the bottom of the curve, you could break through barriers with sheer force, but that's not the case at the upper end.

For the first several years of my career, I could go out on my own and get there, but with every year that passes, positioning has become more important as I try to work my way up to the top of the power law curve.

I spend most of my year lining up my dominos to knock one down. It takes much more patience. I usually take two to three big swings a year and hope to connect and spend the rest of my year building up to those moments.

There is good news here, though, because successful people want you to succeed. One of the ways those at the top stay relevant is to find fresh new voices.

However, those at the top are often wary of newcomers. They have worked so hard to build their reputation and know it can be taken away in an instant.

Moreover, they know that for every rung they drop in relevancy, the power law curve works harder against them.

Another hope came with the foundation of platforms like Kickstarter and Substack that allow creators in the middle of the power law curve access to funds they never had until the last few years.

Platforms like these help writers build sustainable businesses, but there is a power law curve even here. There's a power law working at conventions, Kickstarter, and retailers, too.

People often ask me why it seems like they are working hard and not getting anywhere, and it's probably because they've reached the point in the power law curve where they have to do different things to succeed, and it just takes longer to do so.

It's a feature, not a flaw, in the system.

Gary Vee used to say that you should get in at the beginning of every new platform you can, and I didn't understand why, but now I know it's because if you hit the right platform, then the power law curve will help you grow fast and get outsized attention, and that attention helps feed your growth to keep you at the top over time.

On some level, I think it's comforting to know the power law curve exists because it means, in some way, growth is predictable and measurable. I know when I hit a cap on what I can do on a platform, I have to diversify or double down to get to the next level, or I have to be happy with the level I am at.

I also know that everything is relational, so if I want to affect change, I need buy-in from people who already have gathered exponential support over the mean creator on a platform. Showing I am an asset rather than a liability can help them grow as well.

I also know that by helping everyone, eventually, some of those people will rise to the next level and become powerful assets in my network.

Yes, that's a bit Machiavellian, but I am only cryptic and Machiavellian because I care, as Taylor Swift says.

THE SCALE YOU NEED TO HIT IS ABSURD

Writers generally charge between $5 to $10 for an ebook and $15 to $20 for a print book. If you're looking at a subscription, the most common subscription is $5/mo or $50/yr across subscription platforms.

Kevin Kelly wrote a piece on his blog in 2008 called " 1,000 True Fans," which became one of the definitive pieces on building an audience with its claim that if an artist can find one thousand people willing to spend one hundred dollars a year on their work, then they can successfully make a living on their art. Even though I have issues with this theory, I hope we can all agree that generating $100,000 in income would make a successful year. The idea is that if you can find 1,000 people willing to give you $100/yr, then you have a six-figure business. You'll need close to 2,000 people willing to pay you $50/yr to make $100,000 in revenue, not profit. Let's talk about that number for a minute, though, because to find 2,000 people willing to pay you $50/yr, you need to "kiss a lot of frogs", as they say, not everyone is a possible fan, which means you probably need to spread your message to 10x more than that to attract enough people to make these numbers work. ***That's between 500,000 and 1,000,000 people to find 1,000 buyers.***

In my own business, 30-50% of buyers will buy again, and 10% will become superfans. ***That means now I need to find 10,000 buyers to find 1,000 superfans and, thus, talk to 5-10 million people.***

I talked to a creator recently who related a story from a company he worked with, where they gathered 4,000,000 to find 100,000 engaged fans and 1,000 of them to become buyers.

They were selling a wildly expensive enterprise product of some type, but even as an extreme example, it's instructive.

The fallacy inherent inside the 1,000 True Fans parable is that you will need to talk to more than 1,000 people to find enough people who resonate with your message to financially back you.

We haven't even included your churn rate in that number, which is the number of people who leave your audience in any given year, which can be 10% or higher. The average churn rate for a SAAS company is 3-8%, which means even in the best companies laser-focused on retention, some people are leaving their ecosystem every month whose revenue needs to be replaced.

However, there is good news here because this is just a math problem now. Every time you wonder why you're not doing better, you can ask yourself if your message has been seen by 5-10 million people. If not, you must chip away at that number a little at a time.

I should mention right here that if you're running a client-based business, this is completely different. If you're a coach or editor, you write for companies or have set up a business where you only need a few clients to make your year, then you can probably get by with word of mouth alone.

I know lots of authors who get by very nicely with a few clients at a time. However, we're not talking about that type of business. We're talking about building an audience that will support your creative writing.

In my own experience, I needed to gather roughly 200,000 emails to find 20,000 engaged readers and 2,000 buyers who financially support my career. Every time I tried to scale above 20,000, my open rates dropped precipitously, but I maintained 20,000 easily once I got there.

I've been able to support myself as a six-figure creator since 2017 with an audience that has mostly stayed loyal during that time. Yes, people leave, but new people come as well.

Now, many people on Substack say that up to 10% of readers will pay for your content, and I've never found that to be true in all my work.

I find it closer to 1-2% across all my platforms. Monica Leonelle and I were talking recently, and she said that to sell 20,000 copies of a book via retailers, you need to give away close to a million copies of your book.

If you're selling those books for $5, then 20,000 copies is $100,000. She's been working with retailers longer than me, and I trust her data.

When working in non-fiction, you can offer things like coaching, courses, or any number of things to help generate more money from fewer people or to fuel faster growth.

When you're building a creative writing business, though, all you have is a $5 book, so growth is much, much harder.

This is why so many authors write in long series. If you have ten books, that's $50 you're making on the same series.

Businesses usually die when they try to scale because their open rates go down, and they don't have a strong enough funnel to turn those readers into buyers.

Companies raise millions in funding to scale because the marketing costs are astronomical.

As you scale, you start to find more and more people who have already tried your work and made a decision about it, so finding new readers becomes increasingly harder over time.

On top of that, we constantly worry about churn, which is the number of people who leave our audience. The average churn rate is between 2-8%, and it looks like, on Substack, the churn rate of paid users might be as high as 15%-20% after six months.

That means every year, as much as 30%-40% of paid members will stop their membership. At that rate, if we don't keep growing, then we'll have zero members after three or fewer years.

There is an opportunity here because scaling is much cheaper for a creative fiction writer than for any other type of business.

Why?

Because it's so hard to do, almost nobody even tries it. Many businesses see trial costs as much as $150, but we can probably find people to try our Substack for $1-$2 or maybe even less.

We can probably get people to download our books even cheaper if we focus on finding the 1% out of those who will buy our book for the long haul.

Additionally, if we start to use platforms like Kickstarter and focus on more pillars of direct sales, we can monetize our audience even more effectively.

I do find that people who resonate with creative fiction are often more loyal than other readers because it's so hard to find people who resonate with the same frequency of weirdness as them.

I'm not saying this to freak you out, but I'm sure it isn't helping. I'm telling you because this is just math, and simple math at that.

If you can see the scale of the problem and the opportunity it presents, it becomes manageable, though hard.

Most things are not a failure of a writer but a failure to understand the problem and make decisions that solve it.

For instance, if you want to take advantage of Substack's recommendation engine, it behooves you to make a publication that is most tailored to utilizing that engine.

It also hopefully makes you stop beating yourself up if you don't want to do this stuff.

Most authors don't want to do any of this stuff, but they beat themselves up all the same. If you don't want to do any of this stuff, it's okay, but please stop berating yourself.

Companies scale by putting an absurd amount of money into growth. Authors scale because they hit the right trope at the right time and doubled down on it.

Even if you don't hit the tropes and get organic growth, you can scale by doing the same things that big companies do but on a smaller scale.

We can have nice little lifestyle businesses that support us creatively without doing much of this stuff, but this is why it's so hard.

It's so hard because it's so hard for everyone. Some people make it look easy, but they are also kicking and screaming to keep it all going before the house of cards comes tumbling down.

There is always opportunity in doing hard things though. If you take nothing else away, at least take that one piece of wisdom and carry it with you.

THE UNIVERSE IS DUMB, AND CAPITALISM IS NONSENSE

I recently learned about Gödel's Incompleteness Theorems, and it helped me put many things into place about how the universe operates. There are many big words that can tell you all about the theorems, but it boils down to the fact that every provable math theory has elements that are unprovable inside of it.

That's nonsense.

So, to prove anything in the universe, you must use elements you cannot prove?

That is the dumbest thing I have ever heard, yet it is true, or at least as true as anything can be in a dumb universe.

When you add that to the fact that the entire fabric of the universe breaks apart when you dig down to the quantum level and realize that quarks…don't do anything we think they will do, you come away with one conclusion.

The universe is dumb and unknowable.

However, that doesn't work to comfort most humans because we are "rational creatures". We must impose order on chaos.

Enter capitalism, which is very dumb but is at least dumb in predictable ways.

And that is the beauty in all of this idiocy. The whole universe, all of existence, is dumb, but it is at least dumb in predictable ways.

While it is infuriating to know that the universe defaults to idiocy, at least if it consistently defaults to idiocy in the same ways, we can make some predictions about how certain things will operate.

Those predictions, while very dumb, create patterns that come to fruition repeatedly. We can model that to have our success if we have robust data sets.

Our whole economic system is built upon this shaky belief that we can impose order on chaos. It's nonsense that goes down to the money we use daily.

The paper in our pockets and the digits in our bank accounts are not tied to anything tangible. They used to be tied to gold, but those days are gone.

Globally, we are in debt of 235 trillion dollars. ***To whom?*** If we're in debt to each other, then shouldn't that at least even out to zero?

Nonsense.

The only thing that keeps our entire economic system afloat is the belief that our money has value.

It is hope that binds us, but we pretend it is more than that to get from the beginning of the day to the end of the day without freaking out completely every minute of it.

The only reason we can exchange currency between countries is because we have all agreed X dollars is equivalent to Y euros.

That is nonsense.

Runaway inflation is just a bunch of people imposing their will that the paradigm has changed, but nothing has changed but our beliefs.

Nonsense.

When you examine this with any level of rigor, it falls apart.

Why does an ebook cost the same as a cup of coffee, even though it takes exponentially longer to make and read a book?

Nonsense.

But predictable nonsense.

People hold themselves back because they need to understand the nonsense in a deep, unknowable way, but that is madness. You cannot answer why a raven is like a writing desk because there are no answers.

It is nonsense.

This nonsense has pissed me off for years, and it will probably piss you off, too, if it's the first, or even 100th, time you have encountered it, but it is the truest thing I have ever said in my whole life.

You cannot understand why nonsense works. You can only hope to perform an action and understand what happens.

We can understand the cause and effect, but why does a red button lead to a higher click-through than a blue one on your homepage?

No idea. ***It's nonsense.*** Experts try to tell you they can make the unknowable knowable, but they cannot. They can tell you the result of an intended action and how to achieve that result predictably, but that is not the same thing.

I started to have sustained success when I became comfortable understanding that something happened and how to repeat it without diving into the why behind every little thing that prevented me from moving forward.

This won't make you feel all warm and fuzzy inside because we are logical creatures. We want answers, but the opportunity here to fall backward and embrace the nonsense.

We are held back by our need to know. I see it all the time. People must know what's on the other end of taking action, even though it's impossible. They leave career-changing money on the table because they think if they research a little more or find just the right data, it will give them the answer.

There are no answers. There is only nonsense. The nonsense is your friend as long as that nonsense is predictable.

I have no idea who will resonate with this post, but I know that if I disseminate it widely, I can touch at least one person.

I have no idea who will buy a book I release, but if I do the same marketing actions I've done for years, then a critical mass of people will buy it.

That's the crux of being in business, but creatives make it much harder than it needs to be.

That coffee is $5 because it is the price the shop can sell to maximize its profit and remain in business.

It's nonsense, but it's at least predictable. That's all we can ask because it's all we will get.

This is why you are freaking out all the time. You are fighting against the chaos instead of letting it envelop you.

If you join the madness and let it wash over you, you can learn to laugh at the nonsense instead of being petrified.

It's hard to allow that unpredictability into your life, but if you can plan for the unknowable by relying on the predictable, it becomes much more fun.

I freak out a lot, too, but when I catch myself, I know it's all a big cosmic joke, making it bearable.

One of the problems with growing a creative business is that if you keep doing what you're doing, people might get bored and tune out. If you change something or anything, people might get bored and tune out.

But you have no idea which is which or when to do either. People like new things when they want new things and want old things when they want old things.

People change on a whim, often within hours or minutes of each other. They will be mad at you if you evolve and angry if you keep doing the same thing. They will love you if you do a new thing and love you if you do an old thing.

All I know is that whatever you do, people want you to do the other thing and the same thing. You have to hope you make good choices on aggregate that people resonate with more than they don't. Tim Ferris likes to say that he hopes each episode of his podcast resonates with 25% of his audience so that every month, 100% of his listeners are happy with at least one of his episodes.

It's helpful to think about but also nonsense to implement. To do the work of marketing and sales, it helps to understand that all of it…well, it's all a bit silly, really.

You are trying to find new readers by doing things that have nothing to do with producing work for those readers to enjoy.

It's quite a lot of nonsense. It's very hard to break your brain enough to fall in love with this kind of work.

It almost requires you to cleave your brain in two and reconstruct it in ways that don't make much sense.

It helps to read Camus and fall in love with Dali. Dadaism and Absurdism are requirements for any creative to learn marketing and sales.

Once you understand that it's all a bit of nonsense and that the universe is just a bunch of bits of nonsense stacked on top of each other, then it all becomes easier.

I am sympathetic if you think it's dumb nonsense. I agree with you. I also believe there is value in that dumb nonsense, and sometimes there is joy in it, especially if you embrace the absurdity of it.

It's hard to do this work, but it's not impossible.

Headwinds are going against you, but in those situations, we lower the sail and start to row.

If we don't have oars, we turn the sails against the headwind and find another path. If we're smart, we have a motor that can propel us forward with minimal effort until we get through the storm.

I don't think it's impossible to build an audience on Substack. I don't think you need an audience from another platform to be successful.

It helps.

I brought over 25,000 subscribers to Substack, and that helped...

...but I built those subscribers from zero. I started building my list from scratch in 2014, and we all start from scratch somewhere.

People like to say, "Oh, it's easy for them because they had an audience", but every one of us built from nothing at some point.

Also, having a social media platform doesn't help all that much in building a mailing list. Pulling people from a platform to your mailing list is an incredibly hard and frustrating task. I've seen countless creators fail at it.

Still, it does help, but it is not required.

I've watched hundreds of my friends and thousands of creators dial their businesses in and break through to the other side of success, growing from an audience of one.

The system is stacked against you, but there are ways to hack the system. Every system has backdoors, and because the universe is so dumb, they are relatively easy to exploit if you know where to look.

I didn't know where to look for a long time. I fought the headwinds and lost a decade of my life doing it.

It took me from 2004-2014 to figure out how to make any money doing this work, and then three more years before I could make a career out of it.

Still, it wasn't until 2020 that I felt comfortable with the uncertainty and confident in my ability to make money doing this work repeatedly for the long term.

That's over 15 years from starting this work to being able to find some stability under me.

Do I think it will take you that long? Gods, I hope not, but *that depends on how stubborn you are about fighting a headwind that only gets stronger over time.*

I was unsuccessful for so long because I thought I knew better than everyone else. It wasn't until I swallowed my pride and got a job in sales to learn what I didn't know that things turned around.

I got an education on that sales floor and rose to sales manager of the department in under a year. How? *I swallowed my pride and learned from other people.*

Taking those strategies and modifying them for my own business was the first time I had success.

Not everything I tried worked, but for every 10 things I tried, one stuck with me. Over time, I started building a stack of skills that worked for me and platforms that consistently brought me money.

If you can find 1-2 strategies a year that work for you, then in a couple of years, you'll have a pretty successful business.

The reason I'm so bullish on learning sales and marketing is because they changed my career. I couldn't sell anything before I learned this stuff. Now, I can sell even my weirdest books because I know how to speak the language of readers.

The books didn't get any better. I got better at talking about them in a way that resonated with readers.

Back then, no legitimate publisher was willing to give me a shot. I had to create my shot, and the tactics I have learned along the way are the only reason I can still do this work.

Make no mistake, it's still very hard, even now. An audience does not suddenly make things magically perfect. It helps, though.

One of the big fallacies about success is that once you have a list or make good money, you have it made in the shade, but that's not true, either. Most successful creators are only successful for a short time and then lose relevance.

If you look at a creator's revenue after they had a massive hit, they almost always have a huge drop in sales within the first two years after it.

Sustained success is very rare in this business. The ones that maintain keep learning what works and how to grow each year.

It is much harder to keep an audience than to grow one in the first place.

When you start, nobody has made their mind up about you. As you grow, more people choose to love your work, but others also decide that you're not for them, making it harder. It makes it more expensive. It makes things much more exhausting.

When I started, I thought that if I hit 10,000 people on my email list, my life would be made in the shade, but it's not like that for 99.99999% of us.

Once I had an audience, the harder work began because I had to keep those interested and engaged while finding new people who resonated with my message.

Every year, I lose 5-10% of my audience, so I must replace it with new people. There are fewer new people with every passing year because I have already met so many of them.

This is not a complaint, but I see many people who misunderstand success, and the truth is that it gets harder over time, not easier. If you find a creator who can succeed year after year, they are a true wizard.

Not that new creators aren't also great to learn from, but you should be open to learning from everyone and not discount a successful creator for being "out of touch".

I thought at some point I could rest on my laurels, but I'm busier now than at any other time in my life trying to keep up with new projects and keep the creative spark alive while continuing to satisfy my audience.

Not everything you learn will resonate, and that's okay. Growth is mainly testing many things and finding the ones that resonate with you. I've tried a million things in my career and found a few that work for me.

I've tried a half dozen subscription platforms that didn't work before landing on Substack. I've been trying to build a subscription audience for a decade, and even though I had an audience, it didn't work until I came here.

Because of that, I appreciate that so many people are open about their growth. I read every growth post I can find on any platform. I know that I learn a lot from them, whether they are from long-time creators or new ones. I learn from the 100 subscriber success stories and the 500,000 ones, too.

It's all data, and it all helps. I don't know what will click, but if I keep inputting data, eventually wisdom will emerge.

You have to act as a filter, but the data is not good or bad. It is input for your brain to process to make better decisions.

Can it bum you out? *Sure.*

Is it exhausting to think about growth when all you have to do is write? *Yes.*

Is that all part of it? *Yup.*

For the first time in recorded history, regular people from all over the world have a real shot of making a living from our creative work and that's incredible.

It's hard, though, and there are headwinds working against you. You should know those headwinds exist so you don't beat yourself up when you run into them.

HOW TO THRIVE AS A WRITER IN A CAPITALIST DYSTOPIA

I have a secret. It is a deep-seated shame in my life.

I desperately want to be one of the cool kids. *I want* to want **to want** to be okay with my status in the world, but I can't stop myself from looking at every cool writer and saying, "I wonder if they would like me".

No matter the space, whenever I enter somewhere new, I desperately seek the validation of the cool kids.

This is even more shameful because I have spent a big part of my life telling people to go their own way and follow the beat of their own drum.

I try to follow my own advice, but no matter how much I tamp down my imposter syndrome, I can't stop that 16-year-old "mean girl" in my head telling me Becky doesn't like me and Georgie thinks I'm fat.

I am a rebel, dang it. It's right there in our mission statement at Wannabe Press. The first line is *We write for the rebels*, yet every act of rebellion I make is followed by a deep-seated hope that the cool kids will validate my existence.

I don't even care if they like me. I want them to say that I was useful. Even if they used me and spit me out, it would probably be okay. I want to sit at the end of their table, even if they don't talk to me.

It is deeply toxic.

So, when Monica took my work and incorporated it into her Book Sales Supercharged series, I found myself saying, *"Wait, the cool kids want to sit with me? Have I finally made it?"*

Even before we became business partners, I knew Monica as one of the foremost thinkers in the publishing industry, and nearly everyone I talk to agrees with that sentiment. I always get people who say, "You work with Monica? I love her!"

Well, that's not true. Usually, when I say she's my partner, the reaction I get is, "You're married to Monica Leonelle? I love her!"

And no, *we are not married*. Monica has a very lovely family. I have a wonderful wife whom I love very much. We live thousands of miles apart from each other. We work together, though, trying to build Writer MBA into a juggernaut in the indie publishing space.

I can't lie, though. A lot of that drive to lead the space fulfills that deep-seated need to be a cool kid myself. *That desire is so bad that my first instinct is to do work for free if I think somebody is cool so they'll like me.*

I'm 40 years old, and I constantly have to keep my 12-year-old fat kid outcast self in check.

Meeting with the top executives in the publishing space and having high-level meetings about how we can work together to move the industry into the future is wild to me after a career spent on the outside desperately seeking enough validation from my peers to be taken seriously.

I feel like I am, for the first time in my life, at the "cool kids" table. I thought it would somehow validate my existence when I was finally taken seriously, but I've learned, above anything else, that the people I was sitting across from in those meetings were as interested in having their ideas validated as I was in having mine taken seriously.

It turns out that almost everybody is looking to be validated by somebody, no matter how successful they look from the outside. ***Realizing that destroyed any notions I ever had that some people naturally have it together.***

I watch many teen movies because I'm perpetually trapped in 1998, trying desperately to understand my high school self. One of the most interesting shifts in the past 20+ years is watching how the "cool kids" have moved from being portrayed almost exclusively as perfect villains and unsympathetic bullies to often being seen as victims in their own right, forced to put on armor to protect themselves from the same worries that everyone else has in their school.

All they want, at the end of the movie, is for somebody to let them take off the heavy armor and exist in the world as a "good" person...but they don't know how to shed the constant need for their twisted form of validation.

That is a cold truth for the rest of us, too. I don't think people would give a flying fart about whether the "cool kids" thought their ideas were good if they had some other way to get objective validation that they were, somehow, intrinsically and without question, a good person that deserved to exist.

And that is bonkers because, if you ignore everything else I ever write, please internalize this: *you deserve to exist as much as any single human on this planet simply by being born.*

Our modern society tries hard to strip you of that simple fact, but that doesn't make it any less true. *You have as much right to take up space and live without fear as any human who has or will ever exist.*

Unfortunately, the capitalist nightmare we currently find ourselves caught up in works every moment to convince us that that isn't true. *It equates being "good" with having money.* So, to prove we are "good", society tells us that not only do we need to have a good idea and convince people our ideas are good enough to earn their attention, *but that we can't truly be a morally good person unless people spend money on what we have to offer.*

Without that commodification of attention, you are judged as lacking true moral worth or, worse in the eyes of society, wasting your time. There is no greater sin in the eyes of today's society than failing to operate at peak productivity. After all, time is money, right?

If you can sell your idea to people, you are good…at least for as long as people keep buying that thing. If not, you are discarded as irrelevant until you can develop something that commodifies attention properly.

The problem is that almost no idea is ever "good" for long, and even if it were an unquestionable truth of the universe, a good idea has no bearing on whether you are a good person or deserve to exist (***because you do***).

That was a crushing thing for me to learn. I always thought that if I just thought about a solution with enough rigor for long enough and could prove my ideas were objectively helpful to people, then maybe I would finally be a good person. When that bubble popped for me, it sent me into a dark place.

It turns out that even if an idea is "good" because it is objectively and momentarily correct (***which, how could you judge whether something is correct when advice needs to be individualized for each person?***), it probably won't be correct very long.

It may be a week, a month, a year, or even longer, but eventually, market conditions will change as people evolve their habits to incorporate your ideas into their workflow, and your idea's worth will erode to virtually nothing in the eyes of society at large…

…which forces you back into the grind to create a new idea that people will think is good enough so that society will pay to adopt it and validate that you are still a good person…

…until they deem it worthless and spit you back out into the trauma cycle once again. It's planned obsolescence on a societal scale.

Still, this is the society we were given, which begs the question of whether it is even possible to put something creative into a world as messed up as the one we've built without constantly succumbing to a crippling degree of depression, anxiety, and despair every waking minute of the day? ***To that, I answer with a resounding maybe.***

I started Wannabe Press after my first Kickstarter campaign, which raised over $5,000. I was not successful as a creative human at the time. That money was the most I had ever made on any creative project I had launched. Before then, the only money I ever made as a creative came from working on somebody else's vision.

It didn't fundamentally change my money situation then, but it changed my relationship with it for the rest of my career. That one glimmer of hope that I might not be wasting my life and our money on a fevered dream was everything to me. *It showed me I wasn't an abject failure.*

After sending money to the printer and settling all the bills from the campaign, I had just enough seed money to start a new company.

Wannabe Press wasn't my first company, mind you. I had launched three failed companies before that moment: [Insert Name Here] Productions, RPN Photography, and BNS Media Group.

All miserable failures, every one of them, for different reasons.

[Insert Name Here] Productions failed because my partner and I were at different stages of our lives and could not see eye to eye. *RPN Photography* failed because I got into a bad car accident and could no longer handle the long, grueling hours on set shooting photos for clients. *BNS Media Group* failed because I moved across the country, and again, my business partners were all on different pages about how much we could devote to the company.

So, this was my fourth creative business venture, and I needed it to stick. I had already started working in B2B sales and was getting pretty good at slinging phones to corporate clients, but I didn't want it to be the rest of my life.

Some creatives are great employees. They love working a stable job and then use that stability to make whatever they want. T.S. Eliot was one of those types.

I am not. ***I barely like taking orders from myself, let alone a boss.***

So, I founded Wannabe Press in October 2014 based on a logo I had from a failed comic project I loved but never got off the ground past a few pages.

We launched officially in February 2015 when I released *My Father Didn't Kill Himself, The Little Bird and the Little Worm*, and *Ichabod Jones: Monster Hunter* on the convention circuit.

I didn't even have the official *Ichabod Jones: Monster Hunter* print run from China yet. I was still printing books in short runs of 25-50 copies for shows because I couldn't wait to start building my business.

I figured that after the success of the campaign, it would be smooth sailing for me.

This is when expectations smashed headfirst into reality. It was harder than I ever thought possible, and worse than that, for every dollar I made, I spent two dollars keeping the company running.

Worse, in June of that year, a couple of weeks after receiving a palette of books and shipping them off to backers, I left my job as a sales manager (***making good money for doing very little***) due to irreconcilable differences with my bosses. I always planned on leaving my job, but not for at least another year.

Still, necessity is the mother of invention, so I dove headfirst into building a company from scratch without knowing what I was doing.

I had a bit of money to burn, but not enough to last more than a couple of months, and I was spending roughly twice what I made to stay in business. In those days, I would joke with my wife that my success was destroying my company.

When you spend $200 only to make $100, you can eat that loss, especially when you have a job. However, when you're spending $20,000 to make $10,000, especially without a job to supplement those losses, *it becomes harder and harder to exist with every sale you make.*

Back in those days, I was mostly kept in business because Ingram would constantly mess up my orders and have to send me replacements. So, I would keep getting hundreds of free books to make up for all the mistakes in my orders. *I knew that couldn't last forever, though.*

I had completed production on several projects while working, which kept me in business for the next year, but that backlog was dwindling. I needed something to change quickly to stay in business…

…which was when I met Mike Kennedy from Magnetic Press. He was a friend of my then-agent. He used to be the publisher of Archaia and had just gone out on his own, well before his company was bought by Lion's Forge or his massive success with Kickstarter.

Back then, he was just a guy with a brand-new company trying to make it work. We met at San Diego Comic-Con in

2016 to exchange notes, and that is where I saw something that changed my whole life.

You see, Mike printed all of his books exclusively in hardcover. He didn't have the size of Dark Horse or the pedigree of Humanoids, either. He was just a guy who loved books and yet was printing the most beautiful books I had ever seen.

Then, he blew my mind when he said something along the lines of, "You know, people think hardcovers are way more expensive to produce, but from the right printer, it's only about $0.80 more a book, and you can sell it for $10-$15 more."

My jaw fell to the floor like in a Bugs Bunny cartoon. If I could spend $0.80 more and make $10 more every book, my spending $1 to make a $2 deficit would immediately flip into a profit.

In my life, I am always looking for leveraged opportunities like this, where one well-placed bet can completely change the whole trajectory of your existence.

When I got home from the show, I did many hours of research to make sure everything Mike said was correct and would work for my business. I ran all the numbers and poured over spreadsheets to ensure the math worked. I studied data for longer than I ever thought my patience would allow.

I can't overstate that *this was a measured and calculated decision*.

I didn't just decide to spend a large portion of our life savings without looking at it from every angle. *I had been selling both of them for years at that point.* They each had their publishing deals (*which fell apart but proved other people saw something in the work they could make money on*) and had sold hundreds of copies each. The only problem was they were costing me too much to print to make a profit. *If I fixed that one issue, it became very clear that everything else would fall into place.*

When I was certain, I convinced my wife that we should risk most of our savings on hardcover books for *Katrina Hates the Dead* and *Ichabod Jones: Monster Hunter.* Eventually, she agreed to support my decision, even though it was a monumental risk since nobody else was doing it.

This one decision changed the entire arc of my life. Those hardcover books let me stay in business while so many people around me flamed out…

…and everybody told me it was a terrible idea when I went to them for what I thought was near-certain validation that I had finally proven my quality as a good human with good ideas.

After I ran the numbers a dozen ways and convinced my wife that printing in hardcover was the only way to save the business, I figured I should ask some other comic book people if they thought making indie comics in hardcover was a good idea.

Now, mind you, these were professional comic people launching indie comic books regularly, *and they all told me I was an idiot for even considering hardcover.*

Even after I showed them the data, they shook me off and told me it would never work. They said things like, "People don't want hardcover comics", "Nobody would pay $30 for a graphic novel", and "The industry isn't ready".

These were smart people who looked at the same data I poured over and gave me the 100% wrong advice for me.

Maybe keeping the status quo was the right decision for them, but it was terrible advice for me. These were the "cool kids" of indie comic publishing, and they were simply wrong. *I would have been out of business in six months if I listened to them.*

Even all these years later, I still can barely believe the transition to hardcover worked to save my business. *My gut was right.*

It should have been a great moment of clarity that proved seeking validation from other people was a fool's errand. Instead, I became even more desperate to get the "cool kids" to admit that my ideas were good and that I was a truly good person worthy of existing.

So, I became the test dummy for the publishing industry.

I told other creators *I didn't care if I was a shining example or a terrible warning as long as other people learned something from me that helped them succeed.* I was willing to destroy my own business so people could step over me to get ahead, even if I went broke or died in the process.

I turned myself into a guinea pig for all the wrong reasons. Whenever somebody told me something was a bad idea, or wouldn't work, or couldn't work, I almost always decided to give it a try, often at my own expense.

Plenty of times, they were right to be skeptical. I often knew it was a terrible idea, yet I tried it anyway. More than once, I ran at full speed straight into a brick wall because I desperately wanted people to like me.

I needed their validation, *and I suffered for it.*

Through that desperation, though, something wonderful happened. *I learned what worked for my business faster than the other authors around me.* With every successive test, regardless of whether it was a success or a failure, I moved forward faster than before. Over time, I leaped ahead further and quicker than almost anyone around me.

I realized that running tests on my business gave me more clarity than waiting for somebody else to validate me ever could.

My tests only bore fruit a very small percentage of the time, but even the failures told me what not to do, which ended up being just as important as the ones that worked out.

It turns out you don't need that many tests to work out to become wildly successful. If even one out of every hundred works out, you can stack those positive outcomes on top of each other and turn that little pile into a business that works for you.

I built a successful company despite myself.

If my constant need for validation hadn't forced me to take action, I would have spent years listening to people tell me what didn't work instead of trying it for myself. By (*accidentally*) taking my career into my own hands, I learned what doesn't work for me and why it doesn't work, which is more precious than gold.

After over a decade in this business, I know, at my core, what serves me, whether people validate me or not. Don't get me wrong, *I still want their validation rather desperately,* but I now know how to survive without it.

So, if the "cool kids" can't validate our existence, who can validate us?

It's us.

We have to validate and motivate ourselves.

Most people I encounter begin their creative life focused on external motivations. They want to be actors because of a desire to walk the red carpet and make lots of money; they want to paint so they can be displayed in the Met or the Louvre; they want to work for Marvel because millions of people will see their work and recognize them.

People motivated by external factors, however, quickly fade out. Let's face it: most artists will never be on exhibit at a prestigious gallery, work for Marvel, or achieve any fame. This realization hits people like a ton of bricks, and they run away without ever looking back.

There is a powerful YouTube compilation where celebrities like Lady Gaga, Russell Brand, and Eric Clapton talk about external motivation. It's called "Celebrities Speak Out on Fame and Materialism" by Think for Yourself. It's a harrowing video, as dozens of celebrities discuss how relying on external motivations to validate your life is a hollow pursuit. ***The only true way to succeed and be fulfilled is to be internally motivated*** by the love of creating something. This is the second type of motivation, internal motivation.

Being internally motivated means your validation comes from the satisfaction of creating something, not from somebody appreciating it. It means you can motivate yourself instead of relying on other people to motivate you. It's a bonus when others appreciate your work, but the true validation comes from making it in the first place.

I've always believed I would die young. That has always motivated me to create a body of work before I died. I was fueled by anxiety for years because I didn't think I could create a large enough body of work to matter in the grand scheme of things before I kicked the bucket.

However, in the last year, that changed when I completed what I consider a substantial body of work. I finished four enormous series (*The Godsverse Chronicles, Ichabod Jones: Monster Hunter, Cthulhu is Hard to Spell*, and *The Obsidian Spindle Saga*) I worked on for over a decade. On top of that, I also released my third solo non-fiction work that compiled the remainder of my thoughts on building a business until this point in my life.

I'm not stopping there, but now that I've built a body of work, there is a stillness inside my soul that I've only ever seen in older creatives. I've always envied the effortless confidence I saw in them and wondered how they could take even the worst moments with a grain of salt.

Recently, I realized they could weather their storms with grace because they are rooted to the ground by the work they had created. *They don't get swept up into the hurricanes of anxiety whipping around because they have a body of work that anchors them.*

It took me 20+ years to build a body of work, but I now believe the secret to creating that stillness in your creative life is to focus on crafting that anchor. *Once you are supremely confident in the body of work on which you stand, nothing can unmoor you.*

If somebody wants to understand me, *they only need to pick up my work and read my thoughts on the page*. The slings and arrows society throws at me, even when it tries its hardest to knock me down, don't phase me nearly as much as they once did because I can always return to the work.

When I have imposter syndrome, I can pull up hundreds of reviews that show I deserve to be here. **When I think nobody cares,** I open a folder on my desk filled with letters I've received over the years telling me how much my work has meant to people. **When I need a boost of confidence,** I see all the books I've created over the years, and it soothes me.

If you want stillness in your creative life, find a way to anchor yourself positively to the body of work you have created. **If you don't have a body of work yet, let that goal be your guiding light.**

The beauty of internal motivation is that it is focused on the work itself. I've been a nervous ball of anxiety for years, but this past year, the anxiety that fueled me for so long has dimmed considerably.

So, if you want to improve your mental health, ground yourself in the work you create. **That's great, but it's only half the equation.** We still need to engage in commerce to acquire a desirable enough resource to exchange for goods and services.

Maybe your solution to the money situation is to get a job that allows you to separate your work from commerce altogether. That's fine. **I know a lot of people who work that way.**

The problem is that even if you can make that work for your creative process, **I've never met an author who didn't want more people to read their work.** If you want more people to read your work, you must get the word out to many people.

Unfortunately, that means doing a significant amount of marketing, and marketing is (often) fueled by money. You can get some readers by focusing solely on free, organic marketing, but the indie publishing industry is increasingly pay-to-play. If you're not spending money, you'll get drowned out, and not enough people will read your work to satisfy you. Without those readers, most authors will eventually get disillusioned and give up. *Looking back at my career, at least 80% of the authors I've ever met have given up eventually because they couldn't find a critical mass of readers, and that's being generous.*

So, even if you don't care about making money on your work, to gather a critical mass of readers to appreciate your work, you'll need to make enough sales to drive your marketing. Sales don't have to be the main goal of your writing, but money is a byproduct of creating value in the world.

On top of that, book design costs money. Covers cost money. Editing costs money. Proofreaders cost money. Websites cost money. How long can you spend money on these things without making anything back before the investment stops being worth it? *It's not fair, but neither is capitalism.*

There is good news, though. *You can still make money without succumbing to the capitalist meat grinder.* The exchange of money for goods and services is not the problem most people have with capitalism. This exchange isn't even capitalism, it's commerce, and there is a big difference between the two. Commerce is the exchange of goods and services and has existed in every society back to the dawn of civilization

Capitalism is a form of commerce emphasizing profit and consolidated wealth built around private, free markets. It is generally categorized by the gluttonous and ceaseless need for endless growth to feed the need for the line to go up. Plenty of scholarships exist, showing that capitalism does not require constant growth to exist…

…but there is no doubt that the nightmarish situation we currently find ourselves in does require perpetual growth. It will, given enough time, devour itself, all the while knowing it is dying by its own hand and being unable to stop consuming anyway. *The feeling you have deep inside your gut that the entire financial system is imploding on itself* is a feature, not a bug, *of the dominant economic paradigm we find ourselves in*…

…but we don't have to design our creative lives around that system to make money. Yes, we have to live in a capitalist system, but we can create an ecosystem more aligned with the values we hold dear inside our businesses. *All capitalists conduct commerce, but not all people who conduct commerce are capitalists.*

While it is debatable whether capitalism can be ethical, there are ways to conduct ethical commerce within the systems forced upon us.

Where is the healthy line between commerce and capitalism? Therein lies the rub because that line is a moving target, and it's personal for each of us.

Some people are more comfortable on the capitalist side of the spectrum , and others prefer to be further on the socialist side of the commerce spectrum. Some might even extricate themselves from the system and rely solely on bartering.

Each decision comes with different constraints and strings attached, influencing how you move forward.

You can make more money as a hyper-capitalist, but the pressure always to perform for the approval of strangers and constantly prove yourself becomes harder to bear as the years wear on you. *A system of bartering is a lovely thought,* but it's hard to exchange a goat for seven pairs of Levi's unless you find the right trade partners, which is why currency is fungible in the first place.

There is no wrong answer, just what is right for you at this moment. *Maybe in your early twenties,* you are happy to delve deep into the seedy belly of capitalism to extract maximum value for yourself to live on later in life. Then, *in your thirties,* you decide that you would rather slow down and take your foot off the gas to preserve your mental health, *and in your forties*, you move to Peru and live in a yurt, knitting and bartering alpaca sweaters.

These decisions don't define our lives, just phases of our lives. One of the ways you can tell we are at peak capitalism is because there is oversaturation in almost every market.

If you follow these things closely, two interesting examples of oversaturation are happening in front of our faces.

1. **Movies.** It's hard to believe, but 20 years ago, there was a thing called the mid-budget movie. These were movies made for roughly $10-$30 million, and they were the workhorse of the film industry. When private equity came to film in a big way, they realized the movies that made the most money were the blockbusters. So, every studio went all-in on them, doubling budgets and creating the crowded summer slate we all see today. When one company does it, it works out fabulously for them, but when one company finds success, others quickly follow. When every company ratchets up the budget on

every movie and then releases it at the same time to a finite audience, they mostly, or all, fail. The box office makes more money now than ever in history, but the fact that every company oversaturated it with huge movies means studios are falling behind.

2. **Artificial intelligence.** We aren't at peak AI yet, but recently, nearly every company I use for my business announced how they integrated AI into their service. It was initially interesting, but now I'm getting 2-3 a day that don't add any functionality I care about to their site. Six months ago, AI was the hot-button issue, and just having it was a big deal. However, can we say that when every website has AI integrated in the same way? Not especially.

In both cases, what's interesting is that there is a flattening out of quality. People expect that just having a summer movie or AI is enough to draw a crowd. While that is true when there are a couple of competitors, it's death when everyone competes with the same tools.

There is a great opportunity for writers here because while everyone competes for the home run or blockbuster, few people service niche markets, and fewer people exist in more fractured, specialized audiences.

To compete in an oversaturated market, you must either "be so great that you stand out over everything else" or "be so niche that you serve a market of underserved fans".

One of the side effects of blockbusters is that they create a market filled with people interested in a specific topic but want to explore parts of it that aren't in the mainstream conversation. This sends them to find different voices that resonate with them and gives you an opportunity to shine.

Mostly, I think we, as authors, need to get a lot better at being scientists. I find that science is a wonderful counterbalance to capitalism. It deals, at its core, with objective truth, which ironically is the exact thing most art grapples with, too. They are widely considered to be diametrically opposed, but I find the opposite closer to the truth.

I'm not saying authors should be making baking soda volcanos (*though I would totally go to that chaos-fueled science fair*), **but I am saying we should apply the scientific method to our author businesses to find the style of commerce that's right for us.** *Will Kickstarter work for your ethics? Should you try direct sales so you're not promoting Jeff Bezos? Will your audience support audiobooks on CDs if they are shipped right to them? Should you start serializing your fiction for free and ask for donations?*

These are questions nobody can answer about your business because your relationship with your readers is unique to you. I can say that many authors do well on Kickstarter, **but some hate it**. I've watched 7-figure authors completely give up halfway through a campaign, and I've watched 3-figure authors take to it like a fish to water.

Same thing with subscriptions. I've seen people make $20k a month on Patreon with their serial fiction and swear it saved their mental health. I've also seen authors in the same genre make $20 a month and have subscriptions destroy their confidence.

There are no hard and fast rules anymore. All of this is possible, and none of it is possible **unless you try it for yourself.**

How do we test? ***Again, carefully and deliberately.***

At Wannabe Press, we tend to break up our year into quarters, which isn't revolutionary since most businesses do it. We plan one new initiative each quarter so we don't overwhelm ourselves. Spending so much time on one thing gives us much time to sit with how it feels for us. I refuse to go very fast with these initiatives. ***That is a line I'm unwilling to cross for my mental health.***

In the first quarter of 2023, we tested a Circle community for fiction. We gave 100% to it, and it ended up a complete and utter failure. We had over 1600 people in our community, and less than 1% were engaged, so we decided it wasn't worth pursuing for the second quarter. We shut it down late last month.

It felt terrible to close the community down so fast, but that is what testing is all about, and I find the process we've created to be immensely fun and fulfilling, both as an artist and an entrepreneur.

I'm not talking about going fast and breaking things. I hate that philosophy, and it was never a very good one to begin with anyway, especially for marginalized communities. The way we test is about going all-in for a limited amount of time to see if we love something, if our audience loves it, and if it fits within the boundaries we've set for ourselves. We still usually fail, but I enjoy trying anyway.

Where will you set your boundaries? Where are you at your best? What makes you comfortable? How will you know if you like something unless you test it against your previous assumptions?

I tend to be at my best during launches. I've tested that assumption 30+ times, and I'm confident that Kickstarter is perfect for me. I do not like to think about money constantly throughout the year. I would rather confine conducting commerce to certain times of the year and spend the rest of it freely giving my work away.

However, if that ever changes, so will my relationship with it. Regardless of how I feel about Kickstarter, it doesn't mean you will have the same relationship with it as I do. We have worked with hundreds of authors to help them launch their projects, *and I can unequivocally say that Kickstarter is not for everyone.*

As somebody who built his name teaching people to use Kickstarter, admitting that feels like a moral failing, but why? *Nothing is for everything.* We live in a world of individualized medicine and individualized education, and that's wonderful. *Why shouldn't book marketing be individualized, too?*

It clearly should be, which means that if something doesn't work, it's not some great moral failure. It doesn't determine your self-worth or your value. It's another failed test on your journey to find what works for you. *You will mostly fail in life if you try to do hard things.*

Then, you have to decide whether you want to improve at those things or give up on them. People say that winners never quit, but that's patently false. Winners almost always quit. They quit things they aren't winning at, which allows them to double down on the actions where they are winning.

I read an article long ago about the joy of receiving 100 rejections in a year because it meant you were trying. If you tried and failed enough times, then you are bound to succeed some of those times. In service of trying, you get better.

The key is to be in the arena enough times for success to find you.

Those who don't do well on Kickstarter often think something is wrong with them, but selling things does not determine your worth. They should commend themselves for even trying anything new. Most people do not try to improve themselves at all. It's hard, and you're fighting against the entropy of the universe itself every time you do it.

For any of this to work, you must try different things until you find the ones that match your goals and then carefully monitor them. If they ever stop aligning with where you are headed, *quit them with reckless abandon*.

If this sounds hard, then you're right; *it is really hard.* It takes an enormous amount of work to exist as a creative human in the capitalist hellscape we live in, which is why I gave such a resounding maybe to the whole idea in the first place.

Over time, I believe finding equilibrium in your relationship with commerce is possible if you work at it. If nothing else, *allowing yourself to understand that this is a long-term process and the odds are stacked against you will hopefully help you stop beating yourself up for not being where you want to be right now.*

HOW TO IMPROVE YOUR MENTAL STATE BY EMBRACING NEUTRAL THINKING

Ever since I was a child, I've wanted to kill myself.

I tried a couple of times, too (and failed, in case you were wondering if I was a zombie or vampire).

Mostly, it was just a lot of ideation.

Constant, insufferable ideation.

The kind of ideation that grows boring in time. The, *Like, I get it, you want to die, but I have to pick my wife up from the airport, so can you cool it for five minutes*, kind of banality usually reserved for a droning teacher from a bad 80s movie.

These pleas for death were not even from my conscious mind, either.

That's the biggest mindscrew of it all. It didn't matter if I was happy, sad, angry, or hungry. If there was a silence of any type or any duration, a little voice would pop up from the depths of oblivion and say, "M*aybe you should kill yourself*".

I listen to a lot of music and podcasts to drown out the silence. I even wrote *The Void Calls Us Home* based on experiences with my inner voice.

It was the dull hum of my life until I reached my late thirties and went to a psychiatrist who told me, "No, that was not normal".

Did you know that normal people don't hear a voice in their heads telling them to kill themselves at all hours of the day and night? I learned this truth several years ago, but it's still bonkers to me.

They **also** told me I was among the most anxious humans they had ever met. So, in total, they told me one thing I already knew and one that blew my frigging mind.

(NOTE: If you hear a voice in your head telling you to kill yourself, that is NOT NORMAL. Seek help. Meds changed my whole existence.)

I went on medication during the pandemic, and guess what? That voice…it vanished.

Well, that's not completely true. It's still there, but it got lazy. I still hear it saying, "Maybe you should…" before trailing off like a drunk aunt at a cocktail party that's blacked out and about to pass out.

As somebody who has had suicidal ideation, severe depression, and anxiety for decades, I have a lot of feelings about positivity.

Mainly, I really, really despise positivity culture. I love optimistic people, especially when they show me tangible opportunities that still exist in the throes of failure, but I do not like positive platitudes or affirmations.

Every time somebody tells me "things will get better", or "to keep a gratitude journal", or some such nonsense, I visualize smashing them across the face with a brick.

It's not very nice of me, and I know they are just trying to help, *but positivity positively grinds my gears.*

This is nothing against people for whom it works, but I am not a positive person…at all. None of that stuff works for me.

Depending on when you started to follow me, the fact that I'm not a positive person might come as a shock. Many people who came into my orbit in the last couple of years have told me I am relentlessly positive.

I don't think that's true. I'm pragmatic, which leads to a generally optimistic outlook for authors in the next five years.

Pragmatically, every author should be able to find a critical mass of fans to sustainable support their work out of a world population of 8 billion people. *Mathematically, it's a near certainty that you can find an infinitesimal percentage of the world's population to resonate with your work.*

That's just data, and data is amazing not because it is positive but because it is objective.

Conversely, if you came into my orbit several years ago, you would know me as a relentlessly negative person.

I'm not really negative, either, though.

I was put in many situations that warped my perception of truth and weighed negatively on my conscience, but after I extricated myself from those situations (*and got on meds*), my mood drastically improved.

There is a grain of truth to both of them, but on any given day, my goal is to be completely neutral. **I'm trying to be very beige these days.**

I have tried every happiness trick and hack in the universe, and while I'm obsessed with happiness to the point of fanatical devotion, I am not happy. I have moments of joy, but I am not, as a rule, jolly.

I could cite studies about happiness until I'm blue in the face, but I don't even want to be happy anymore. Happiness is a whole lot of baggage, and I don't need it in my life.

I just want to be beige. In fact, **I actively try to avoid happiness.**

I have, from a very young age, equated happiness with "bad stuff is about to happen". If good things happen and bad things happen, then it's nothing but a vicious cycle.

I'm not a monster, though. Well, I'm not a monster for *that* reason.

Things can make me momentarily joyous, and I love a wide spectrum of nouns (*your general people, places, things, and ideas*) and a smattering of verbs, too.

I don't run away from my wife, my dogs, my family, or my friends, but I focus on finding moments of joy and love and avoid things that will make me "happy".

I do actively run away from positivity culture, though, because I find what they are peddling is toxic. They are coming from a place of love, and I don't want to ruin their vibe, but that ish is not for me.

Things don't, in my experience, get better.

They get bad in different ways.

Even if 90% of my life is going well, at least 10% is an absolute dumpster fire at any time.

If I'm constantly chasing happiness, and happiness is equated to positive things happening, I will never be happy because bad things will always happen.

It is an unsolvable equation. Even if 99% of things are good, something will go wrong and ruin everything.

Yes, specific bad events can turn around, but life is like a seesaw. If it gets out of balance with too much positivity, then a big, fat blob of yuck slams down and catapults whoever's on the other side high into the air of negativity.

Not to mention that if I plan for things to "eventually" turn around, and then they don't, it makes me spiral into a deep, dark place.

More than anything in the whole world, my goal is to stop myself from spiraling into negativity. I will gladly give up ever feeling pure happiness again if I can avoid spiraling, too.

I spend the whole of my life trying to prevent bad thoughts before they ruin my mood and pulling myself out of a tailspin before I crash into a fiery wreck when they do.

I'm pretty good at it, by and large, and positivity has zero to do with it. Instead, my focus has been curtailing extreme emotions on either end of the spectrum.

By curtailing my happiness just a bit, I've also been able to clip my anger issues (which is a story for a whole different day), my sad thoughts, and my big, bad thoughts.

These days, I try to keep myself as close to the middle of the seesaw as possible.

I thought I was a weirdo who didn't know how to be happy, but somebody told me about neutral thinking, which changed my life. Neutral thinking is about not labeling things that happened as good or bad but simply accepting that they did happen.

Think about this analogy:

A farmer wins a new horse. His neighbor comes over and asks, "Don't you think this is so great?"

The farmer replies, "Maybe".

A farmer's son breaks his leg on the horse. His neighbor comes over and asks, "Don't you think this is terrible?"

The farmer replies, "Maybe".

The farmer's country declares war, but his son avoids the draft because of his broken leg. His neighbor comes over and asks, "Don't you think this is so great?"

The farmer replied, "Maybe".

I have been living this philosophy for years but didn't have a name for it…and it perfectly sums up why I hate positive thinking as much as I hate negative thinking.

I have been to therapy, taken meds, and followed just about every guru under the sun, and this, along with copious medications, is the only thing that has truly helped me.

It seems simple in retrospect, but assigning good or bad to every action is onerous. Most things are not good or bad. They simply are, and coding them on either side of the divide was messing me up.

When I started to reframe stuff simply as existing, I realized that not only were things not intrinsically good, but they also weren't intrinsically bad, either.

I already talked about my dogged determination to prevent spiraling, and the biggest reason for my spiraling has always been thinking bad things were happening and wouldn't stop happening. *Even "being positive" made me see negative things everywhere.*

At my suicidal worst, the voice in my head would pile on as well, and it would feel like I was drowning. Getting on meds helped, but it wasn't enough by itself.

Neutral thinking was the key that unlocked the final door and allowed me to live a semi-normal life.

Now, when something happens, it has no intrinsic value. It doesn't make me spiral because it is not good or bad. It simply happened.

It turns out that if nothing is good or bad, it's hard to see the bad in every decision.

What helped the most was nearly dying last year. After I left the hospital, people sent me well wishes, which was great, but it left some questions I wrestled with for a long time. Was it good that I wasn't dead? Was it better to be sickly than dead? Would I accept existence if I was given the choice?

I eventually realized none of those questions mattered because I did not die, and I was not given the choice not to exist. Since I wasn't going to kill myself, only one truth remained: that I was alive.

It didn't matter whether my death would be positive or negative because either way, I would still be dead, and that would cause a cascade of decisions that people I love would have to make in my absence.

Some decisions would be good, and others would be bad, but it didn't matter because one truth trumped everything else—I wasn't dead. I was alive.

Embracing that simple fact allowed me to frame my life in a new way and inch myself away from the darkest ends of the mental health seesaw, which goes from toxic positivity to toxic negativity at either end.

People have told me my whole life that only a positive attitude could combat a negative attitude, but that is bull plop.

When I was on one end of the seesaw, all positivity did was throw me hard in the other direction toward negativity, which led dramatically into spiraling.

Instead, neutral thinking allowed me to clip off the positive and the negative until I was mostly balanced in the middle of the seesaw.

It allows me to cut off negative thoughts.

Yes, it also clips the positive thoughts, but they never made me happy in the first place. As I mentioned, picturing something positive made me think of all the horrible things that would happen if anything good happened.

That is a losing game.

Besides, it's not so bad being beige. I still experience love and joy, which are the best things anyway, and while I try to surround myself with goodness, positive thinking can go screw.

Last year, I came to Austin on a trip that included seeing a couple of my good friends who moved here. I was lucky to go again this year, around the same time…

…and quickly realized things were much different this time.

Previously, when I stayed with my friends, we enjoyed staying up later than usual and chatting. I was fully available to do things, go places, and engage in these conversations.

This year, I was in a bad way.

My migraines were so terrible that I could barely string two sentences together for most of the time I was with them. After contracting COVID last year, which led to long COVID, I have been slowly degrading into a shell of my former self.

It is…suboptimal.

It's often hard to think straight due to the migraines that have been beating against the inside of my brain in a near-constant state since late last year.

It interferes with every part of my life.

For instance, I always work out when I'm away, clock in an hour or more at the gym, walk 10,000+ steps, or both when I travel. It's annoying how consistent I've been about it in the past years, even spending time at the gym when I went to Vegas for 20Books last year.

However, after a couple of days at the gym down in Austin this year, I was wiped to the point of exhaustion, unable to even keep my head up for the whole day.

This is not uncommon in the long years of my life. I've been chronically ill for 20+ years. Not recently, though. In recent years, I've been better-ish.

I spent years in my 20s and early 30s confined to the couch, unable to do more than a few hours of work every day. I would have worked from about 10 am-2 pm in the years before and immediately after my Graves' disease diagnosis.

After that, I had to sleep for hours, only to get up before my wife came home, and then go immediately to bed soon after dinner.

It wasn't much of a life, and I worked very hard to get healthy. I've never been more proud than when I stopped needing a nap every day of my life.

For years, I felt like a prisoner of my body, but recently, I have felt like my body was a vessel for me to live a real life instead of the other way around.

COVID took that from me…

…, and I am weirdly at peace with it. It's not good or bad, necessarily, but it exists.

It is suboptimal for sure, but whether it is good or bad…I don't know.

In my younger years, I would have railed against my body, cried about my lot in life, and withdrawn from the world to become a bitter husk of a person.

Now, when I had every reason to curse the universe for leaving me stuck in bed while my friends were hanging out at a tiki bar with my wife, all I felt was an inner stillness telling me to withhold judgment until the end.

The end of what?

It's unclear, but it's helping me to avoid spiraling into the pits of depression as I have so many times before, and that is my optimal state.

People always tell me that I have myself together, and that's true to an extent, but there's a good reason behind why that is true and why I don't ever recommend it to others.

I have myself together because if I don't, I lash out at everything all the time. I must avoid stress at all costs if I want to be even mildly tolerable.

I get things done the minute they come in because I can't not and like the person that comes out.

Earlier this month, I was running late, and I turned into a monster. Luckily, I was alone. Still, I felt guilty about it for two weeks.

It's not a choice. I don't think most of the way we go through the world is a choice. The choice is how we want to be seen and how we want to see ourselves.

The rest is constructing the universe around us to allow that best self to exist. We can control how our emotions present, but we can't control having them.

I prefer to avoid the conditions where my worst self has a chance to take over.

For me, that means rigidity and predictability with way more time than is reasonable to finish things or get places before it becomes a problem.

In that world, my best self can exist. The question of good and bad habits is a misnomer, anyway.

Some habits that allow my best self to exist would bring out somebody else's worst self.

I've gotten very good at setting the right conditions for my best self to flourish, but I doubt it would work for anyone else as it does for me.

We all have to set our conditions for success, and that's incredibly personable to each of us.

I know the conditions I must maintain to stay here, and I hate the person who comes out when those conditions aren't met.

That looks like having myself together because the opposite is untenable to me.

IS IT EVEN POSSIBLE TO BE A WRITER AND HAPPY AT THE SAME TIME?

I was hanging out at the LA Festival of Books with my friend, who wrote a choose-your-own-adventure book called *You Are a Filmmaker*. He's a film professor working in the industry for as long as I've known him, and the book has over 100 endings.

After somebody left our booth with the book, I joked with him that I was thinking about writing a book called *You Are an Author,* but it would be wholly depressing because every ending would be "…and you are miserable."

"You've sold a million books…and you are miserable", "You're working at a coffee shop writing your book in the dead of night…and you are miserable", and so on.

I've talked before about how I have big feelings about happiness, but I also don't want to be miserable.

While it certainly seems like the vast majority of my writer friends have been flirting with misery most of their careers, we don't have to be miserable to write, do we?

The concept that the best art comes from tragedy is ridiculous, after all. Lord of the Rings was written by a father telling a story to his son, and it was revolutionary. Whether it is even ethical to profit from tragedy is a conversation I will keep to another day, but there's no doubt that the general scholarship states that we write better when we are sad. When I typed *"Can you be happy to write"*, this was the first article that popped up, titled **Why You Can't Write When You're Happy.**

At the beginning of my career, I was fueled by sadness and tragedy. However, since getting on meds and improving my outlook a few years ago, I've had to change my relationship with my work to continue with it.

It turns out that it's really hard to revisit past work you wrote while suffering suicidal ideation without spiraling again, and that sucks. On top of that, there are few jobs that tell you, "To be good at this, we need you to be miserable".

Even if you are miserable working at Big Box store #3426, their training manual probably has a section about happiness or averting depression. I plan to continue doing this work until I die, and constant misery is not something I can tolerate for the next (hopefully) 40+ years.

So, I did a deep dive into the things that were making me unhappy, and it turns out that it's capitalism, silly. Since I live at the intersection of craft and commerce, I wanted to share some concepts that inform our relationship to making money with our art, how they influence our mindset, and how we can spin them to our advantage when advantageous.

Will that make you happy as a writer? I don't know. I don't think happiness should be the goal, but I hope it will make you less miserable and move the needle closer to neutral. It will certainly make you less bitter.

I had a conversation with a creator a while ago. What we talked about has gnawed at me. It's something I hear all the time. It impedes so many creatives from moving to the next level.

He was bitter because nobody he knew wanted to buy his book.

He went to his audience, hat in hand, and couldn't get anybody to take a chance on what he had to offer. He didn't understand why his family would forsake him while they bought whatever celebrities told them to buy.

"It's not personal," I told him.

"But why?" he asked me. "They are my family. They should be supporting me more than some celebrity."

I only had one reply. "Guilt can't scale."

You can't guilt people into buying something. It makes them bitter and resentful. They see your panhandling as an obligation they want to get rid of as soon as possible. They won't become long-term customers. Even if you somehow get their money, all you've done is make yourself a nuisance. You haven't made a customer for life.

Make no mistake, that's what you are after in the end. One of the biggest predictors of overall success is customer lifetime value. **Obligation does not build a happy customer and is never appreciated.** Think about the things you are obligated to do. You are obligated to pay your mortgage. You are obligated to do chores. You are obligated to take your dog to the vet.

All those things suck.

Nobody willingly takes on an obligation with a smile. You can only force an obligation on somebody. And you don't want to force anybody into buying your product. You want them to buy it happily. You want them to buy all your products because they fill a need in their life, even if that need is edifying their soul.

I have 20,000 people on my email list, and in the past year, I've made fewer than 2,000 sales. *That means at least 90% of the people on my email list haven't bought from me in over a year.*

I could be mad about that. I could sulk. I could cry. I could pound my fist in the air. I could yell at the people who didn't back me.

But what will that get me?

It won't get more people to back my projects. It won't make me more money. All it will do is ruin friendships and destroy family ties. On top of all that, it would make me an angry, spiteful, vindictive man. That's no way to go through life.

So, I leave the 90% alone and focus my products on those who buy. Those are the people who like my sense of humor. They are the ones who resonate with my message. Those people want to buy my products. They have the highest customer lifetime value. They are my target audience. That's no different than every other company. This is how all companies succeed. They focus their message on the small sliver of the marketplace that resonates with their message.

There are multiple ways to increase your profit, but focusing on who isn't buying from you isn't one of them.

You don't want people to buy things out of obligation or guilt. You want them to buy because they *want* to buy.

Those are the people who are in your ideal market. Those are the people you can build a business around. You will never convince somebody your product is cool if they don't see a need for it.

Maybe, along the way, you'll guilt a couple of people into buying from you. ***But those people are only short-term gain.*** They aren't going to buy every one of your products. They aren't in for the long haul. They aren't going to support your entire career.

You will do well to remember that and become okay with it. In the short term, it hurts when your family doesn't buy from you, especially when you are just getting started. In the beginning, you are clawing for every dollar, but that's why strategic planning is so important. That's why you can't focus on the short term. You have to focus on the long term.

And in the long term, understanding that it's not personal is one of the most important skills you can learn for your business and sanity. After all, guilt can't scale.

Now that we've broken down how to nurture the bottom of your sales funnel, let's talk about how to build the juicy middle of it with casual fans. The good news is that while building up your superfans, you will also make money on casual fans.

I've been a six-figure author since 2017, and I'm not even sure I have 1,000 true fans yet.

Maybe you don't need $100,000 to lead a happy life. Even though previous scholarship has said that happiness caps out at $75,000 and recent studies dispute those findings, you may live on much less than that amount. Let's say you want to make $50,000 as a writer to lead a happy life. The latest survey of working writers found they make an average of $12,000, putting you at the high end of earners.

Let us also stipulate that this is after expenses, which include editorial, marketing, and everything else needed to run your business. In this scenario, *$50,000 goes into your personal bank account at the end of the year.*

If you are lucky, you can run your business at a 50% profit margin. If you're a non-fiction author, you're probably laughing behind your 80% profit margin, but for most of my life, I've run a 22% profit margin, *so this is more than double my average*.

That means for every $1 you spend, $.50 is pure profit after expenses. If you want to make $50,000, you need to make $100,000 because an additional $50,000 will be expenses for your business. *It's important to understand that every business has expenses,* and the more you make, the more you spend.

So, you have a $100,000 goal for your business to keep $50,000 for yourself.

An ebook generally sells for $3.99-$4.99. For the sake of this argument, I will say $5 because it's easy to do the math. Most vendors only give you 70% of the total sale price, keeping 30% for themselves.

That means on a $5 ebook, you will see $3.50.

At that price, *you will need to sell 28,571 copies of a book to make $100,000* in revenue. Most people write more than one book a year, so let us assume you write an average of 4 books a year.

If you release four books a year, you will need each book to sell 7,142 copies, at least to make $100,000.

If you release 10 books a year, you will only have to sell 2,872 books to make the same amount of money (though releasing more books eats into your profits). Let's stick with 4 books since that's what most people can comfortably maintain.

The nice thing about books is that ***once you have a good back catalog, you can make as much as 50% of your income from back catalog books alone.*** That means you only need to make 50% of your income from new releases. The more fans you meet, the more you chip away at that number.

It might sound daunting, but it's very doable through marketing and advertising. If you know the numbers, you can work toward them. ***Otherwise, you will keep being adrift in an ocean of uncertainty.***

If you've made it this far into a very data-nerdy article on building a writing business, you are now ready to understand my favorite statistical concept: the Bell Curve.

I have a degree in demographic sociology, so I am intimately familiar with the Bell Curve, as I have worked with it since I was 18.

The general idea of the Bell Curve is that if given enough of the correct data on almost any subject, the data distribution will look like a bell with a big, fat middle that tapers off on the edges. You can get into the weeds about whether this is the correct distribution for every population, but since I look at audience building and sales from the sociological perspective of how large groups behave, it is apt for this discussion.

Why is this important in sales?

Because almost everyone gives up on accumulating data before their distribution fits into a Bell Curve.

What do I mean by that?

Let us say that at a convention, every 100 people you talk to will lead to $100 in sales. Once you talk to 100 people, you can reliably predict you will make that amount of money almost every time.

The reason that is predictable is that you have found the normal distribution of your data.

However, if you give up and only talk to 50 people, you will not reliably make $50 in sales.

Why is that?

Because you have not spoken to enough people to normalize your curve.

You see, if you talk to 100 people, you might make that $100 from the first two people, or the last two people, or somewhere in the middle.

But by skewing your metrics, you no longer have a Bell Curve, which makes your curve more erratic and less reliable.

You might make $300 from talking to 10 people or $0 from talking to 70 people, but it's impossible to predict because you have not collected enough data.

The graph of data eventually normalizes into a Bell Curve because there is enough data, a robust data set, to create such a curve.

This can't be overstated enough. ***If you gather enough data, your data will, 100% of the time, result in a curve that looks like a bell.***

The Bell Curve is the foundational metric of statistics. ***It's how we can poll 1,000 people and make assertions about a whole population.***

There is another factor working here, though, because to get a Bell Curve, you need your data collection to be random.

For instance, you can't pick and choose who you talk to at a convention because that is no longer random. I can't tell you how many sales I've made from people outside my target demographic simply because I talked to them.

So, if you only look for people who look like your perfect customer, your standard distribution falls apart.

This doesn't mean you should go everywhere and talk to everyone, even at a supermarket or swap meet, unless they have a high propensity for being filled with your ideal clients.

For instance, ***if you want to study voting patterns in Texas, you wouldn't poll people in Oklahoma, right?*** So, you need to find the random distribution in whatever population you choose, like a specific convention.

However, it does mean when you decide to do a marketing/sales push, you need to get a robust data set. Otherwise, your numbers will vary wildly.

This concept is a foundational component of all sales. It's how you can predict the ROI of your ad spend, choose what conventions to go to, and how much money you will make next year.

People ask how I can so accurately predict my sales numbers, and it starts with having a robust data set.

When I enter a new situation, what scares me most is that I don't have enough data to assess the situation properly, and I don't trust anyone else's data without replicating it personally.

So, how do you use this? Learn your numbers and talk to more people when you do a promotion.

Send more emails. Run more ads. Talk to more podcasts. *DO MORE THINGS* to better predict your next launch and the next steps.

Your numbers might vary wildly from mine, but you'll be unstoppable once you know what it takes to get normal distribution for your launches.

What if you fail at doing all of this hard stuff? *You likely will, at least with some of this stuff, and that's okay.* Success is built on failure. There are many points of failure that could cause a project to seem like a failure, *but it doesn't mean the project itself is a failure*.

Let us look at marketing a book, for example. Yes, it is possible that the book is horrible. However, if you are running an ad for a book, many pieces could lead to failure, even if the book is great.

For instance, *on the ad level:*

- The ad copy might not be right.
- The targeting could not be right.
- You could be targeting the wrong audience.
- You could have launched at the wrong time of day.
- You could have launched on the wrong day of the week.
- You could be targeting the right audience, but your ad isn't being served to the right people.
- The audience you chose might not be big enough.
- The imagery you are using might be wrong.
- The competition for ads might be higher than normal.
- A more popular book might be targeting the same audience and pulling their attention.

Additionally:

- Ad costs might be higher because of the time of year, like at Christmas, when companies blow their remaining ad budget for the year.
- People might be away from their computers more because it is summer and they are with their families.
- A world event might be diverting attention from your advertisements.

If you can get a great ad that gets people to click, **the fun doesn't stop there**:

- The copy on your page might not be strong enough.
- Your tagline might not be compelling.
- Your cover image might be weak.
- Your cover image might not be aimed at the right market.
- Your blurb might be aimed at the wrong market.

And then, even if you can get somebody to read your book:

- Maybe the first page isn't amazing, and they put it down, even though the rest of the book is great.
- Maybe the book isn't written to market.
- Maybe you have written a book into an oversaturated market.
- Maybe trends have shifted.
- Maybe you haven't created good enough hooks at the end of each chapter.
- Maybe you haven't written a long enough series to earn out your marketing costs.

Those are just some of the things that could happen with a single book that might prevent it from being successful, and if all of those things go perfectly, maybe you will have a hit, but perhaps you won't because some unknown unknown you didn't know about went wrong.

The good news is that you can tweak any and all of these things and relaunch your book or any product again and again until it's right and you find the perfect audience for it. Most projects aren't failures. It's the marketing that is a failure.

I don't watch a lot of sports, but I liked this answer by Giannis Antetokounmpo after he was asked if the whole season was a failure because the Bucks were eliminated from the playoffs in the first round.

Being somebody who has failed does not make you a failure, even if all you have known is being unsuccessful.

Screwing up does not mean you are a screw-up, even if you never seem to get it right.

Current states can be changed and often change quickly and without warning.

You are not one thing. You are many things and have the potential to be anything.

I've been interviewed hundreds of times in my career. In every one, they ask me how I became a writer. I've answered a lot of different ways, but the one I keep coming back to is that I never knew that wasn't what you were supposed to do.

When I was young, everybody was going to be a director, or a writer, or an actor.

I assumed that when I hit 40, everybody would have done that thing. It didn't cross my mind for one second that wouldn't happen.

I was intimidated, frankly, because there was so much talent around me.

Then, life happened, and I looked back 20 years later and realized that just because you wanted to do something didn't mean that wasn't what happened.

I tell people that the great separator is time and effort.

When you're at the starting line, there are millions of people around you, but as you keep doing work, people fall off until you're one of very few, a select group that has kept the creative spark.

You have no idea how rare that gift is until you sit back 20 years after high school and think about all the people who wanted to do something creative with their lives and how few ended up doing it.

Russell Nohelty

There are many aspiring creatives, but so few make it to the mountaintop with their spark intact that it's almost a miracle it ever happens at all.

I'm not saying they aren't happy. Many of my friends who stopped doing creative work are very happy, but they aren't doing the creative thing they set out to do when we were wee babies.

They aren't doing the thing that intimidated me about them for so long.

People more talented than you will fall away. People who boast more will go away. People who you think are guaranteed to win will go off and do something else. Hotshot creators will burn bright, burn fast, and burn away. I've seen it all while slowly doing the work day after day.

My work has never been perfect. Far from it, but I've learned from it every step of the way and kept going. Showing up and doing the best work you're capable of is the secret to the whole game. It's not one or the other. Making one great product doesn't give you a career. Showing up without making something doesn't make a career. Showing up and doing great work consistently makes a career, especially if you can keep showing it to more and more people.

At the end of the day, you will be alone on a mountain, and you'll look around at other mountains and see the people who climbed the summit, and you will bond with them instantly, because they were the survivors.

In this work, most of it is about surviving with the creative spark still inside you, protecting it fiercely, and outlasting other people.

Being a writer is work, and work often sucks. Historically, I have not been a happy person. I suffer from both anxiety and depression. I fight every day against my relentless negativity. However, recently, I set out to change that as much as I could. I decided my new motto was "chase the joy".

I think understanding these concepts allows you to chase joy better in your career. ***If you know you must reach 10 million people to build a successful business, you treasure those who resonate with your message.***

If you know that it's incredibly hard to do this work, then when it shows itself to be incredibly hard, you won't beat yourself up over it too much.

There is joy in the work, though. I didn't know that at first. Everything I did was filled with misery. However, soon enough, I found that interlaced with my misery were moments where the dopamine hit me.

It was only for a moment, but like a ping in a great ocean, I used it as a guide. Every time I felt that dopamine hit, I would try to analyze why I was so happy in that one brief moment.

Over time, I could put together a list of things that made me happy, and even though I was still mostly miserable, I started to chase those moments, whether it was the thrill of a sale or a great review.

I found the things that I loved doing, the shows that resonated with me, and the parts of my job that I enjoyed...and I tried to do them as much as possible. I assumed my revenue would go down as I cut out the miserable tasks I hated, but I made more money this year than I did last year.

And I did it in ways that mostly brought me joy.

Not always, of course. Honestly, *there are still a lot of days that suck*. There are things in business you need to do which just aren't fun. There are moments, even in the fun part, that are miserable.

However, for the most part, I could stretch those moments of joy into whole hours or even days. For me, that's a huge accomplishment.

HOW TO REFRAME CAPITALISM TO MAKE SALES AND MARKETING WORK (BETTER) FOR YOU

It's hard to show writers how to grow their author business without talking about capitalism because the biggest thing holding writers back are the constraints of capitalism.

Specifically, the need for hypercapitalism to commodify everything to extract the most value from it. Most writers start writing in their spare time to relieve the stress of their jobs. It is a release valve, but in our current capitalist dystopia where everything must be commodified, monetizing their work puts it in direct conflict with the original purpose of that work, which was to relieve stress and be an outlet for capitalism.

Authors generally feel gross about marketing and sales because of the way capitalism teaches you to commodify your work. Unfortunately, it is the dominant economic paradigm we live in, so we must soldier on with it.

If I cannot completely disentangle commerce from capitalism, at least I can show you different ways to think and talk about your work and make money that don't feel as gross as capitalism often makes writers feel.

What makes you feel gross about sharing your art is probably not the marketing or the sales…it's the capitalism that forces the revenue line to go at all costs.

So, when people say, "Why does this guy talk about capitalism so much? All I wanna do is find more readers to support my work."

It's because to grow your business, you almost always have to change your relationship with capitalism.

To do that, you must understand that capitalism is everywhere. Once you do that, you can build a better relationship with it and your art. At that point, we can create conditions to live within it.

Capitalism is the dominant economic force of our time. Even if we wanted to escape it, unless we lived in a yurt on a remote island, catching our food and making our clothes, we wouldn't get far without engaging on some level.

Additionally, let's face it: capitalism has its benefits. Besides the fact that a climate apocalypse is currently knocking our door down, things are pretty okay for many of us, especially compared to where we were even a hundred years ago. Depending on the metric you use, capitalism has raised more people out of poverty than any driver in modern history.

Of course, those are the same people who will be climate refugees in the coming years, but capitalism is not without benefits. We live better today than kings did two hundred years ago. Honestly, I would probably take my life over a king's from even a century ago.

That said, capitalism might not be the enemy of artistic expression, but it is certainly not a friend to it, either.

The fact is that capitalism forces almost everything to be monetized and productized, which is antithetical to most people's idea of artistic expression. Sometimes, artists need to follow their muse into unprofitable corners of the world. Capitalism is very bad at allowing us downtime. For instance, we can't have hobbies anymore. We have side hustles, instead, because we have to monetize every action. *It's deeply toxic.*

If we aren't being productive, or if we dare seek stillness, the forces of capitalism rise to say you are wasting time. It's been such a constant message for decades that we have internalized it.

You are constantly bombarded by things you should buy, bills you must pay, or ways to make money to survive. Capitalism is hungry and must be fed, even as it causes hunger and poverty.

Our entire economic system is based on increased productivity and revenue, from the stock market and down. At best, capitalism and artistic expression are frenemies. They aren't going to kill each other on sight, but there is much spiteful sniping and conspiring against each other in private.

Even if we yearn for a better system, the fact is that we live in a world of capitalism in the same way Henry Ford lived in a world of horse-drawn carriages or Nikola Tesla grew up in a world of candles.

We must learn to navigate this world even if we hope to change it. At best, we have to find a way to create a bubble around ourselves to insulate ourselves from the worst parts of our hyper-capitalist society.

Yes, it might only be paper-thin at first, but over time, we can expand that bubble more and more to protect our artistic expression from the worst parts of capitalism.

We can never completely isolate ourselves from capitalism, but we can create a shield around ourselves and our art. What follows are some of my best trips to build barriers between our art and our capitalist tendencies.

The more we want to grow, the more we must engage with capitalism, as it's the dominant force of conducting commerce in the world. So, my plan for this article is to give you some mindset tricks and reframes to help you exist sustainably in this capitalist hellscape while still creating work you care about deeply.

If capitalism forces us to put a price on everything we make in service of "extracting value from our productivity", then giving our work away isn't something we do because our work doesn't have value. We give it away because we value our readership and believe that if somebody reads my work, others will resonate with it and see the value, too.

I often tell people that I'm giving my work away for free/at a discount because I'm making a gamble that you'll love my work enough to buy it at full price in the future.

I'm more than happy to make that gamble a billion times.

In capitalism, *everything we make must have value, but it is our choice how we price it.* We can price our work below, at, or above market value. We can also give it away for free.

That is our choice. That is one small way we take the power back from hyper-capitalist forces pushing against us.

It doesn't matter to me if you buy my books. I think you should buy them because you'll enjoy them, but I am solely concerned that you believe it has value. ***You can't believe that if I don't believe it.***

If we both agree that my book is worth $20, and I sell it for $10, I'm giving you a deal. If I give it to you for free, I've changed the paradigm. This trick completely transformed the game for me. ***It gave me control.*** I always give readers my best stuff, whether it's free, at a discount, or paid in full.

The difference in how I price my work is my choice.

Most people are worried about somebody buying their work, but they are masking the real question that matters:

Do you see the value in the work?

If you and your subscribers agree that your work has value, you're playing a different game.

It's not about selling. ***It's about showing the value until they see the worth and buy.*** Even if they don't buy it, if they see its worth, then that's all I can reasonably hope to influence.

Then the question becomes how much value I need to show you before you buy from me.

By simply agreeing that what we do has value and then giving it away for free, you have extracted yourself ever so slightly from the pressures of capitalism.

The hardest sale for me is the first sale.

Why?

Because once somebody has bought something from you, they have set the price.

That first sale shows that I am not bonkers for believing my work has value. It shows that my work does have worth. It shows I didn't overprice it or completely misconstrue the market.

Now, will there be mass adoption? I don't know. Maybe there are only 100 sales in all of the world. Likely, there are thousands. I just have to find them.

I know that once one person buys at a price, many more people will see the value at that price.

They just haven't...yet.

My job is to convince them of the value. Perhaps they need to know more about what I'm selling. Maybe they need to know me at a deeper level. Perhaps they need more time.

That part I'm not sure about when that first person buys. What I am sure about is that if one person (*preferably not a family member or close friend*) buys from me, then lots more people would be willing to buy from me *if certain conditions are met*.

Writers often take somebody not buying their work as a personal failing, but it's usually not that at all. Most of the time, it's a failure to meet the other conditions necessary to make somebody buy.

In capitalism, money is equated to your intrinsic worth to exist. This is patently absurd, but we've been fed it for so long that we begin to believe it. This is one of the main causes of imposter syndrome as well.

However, if instead we start thinking about that rejection as simply failing to meet the conditions necessary to convince somebody to buy, it stops being about the money.

Now, it's about the connection. Now, it's about the journey. Now, it's about discovery.

If somebody loves my work, they will likely buy if they can, but buying isn't the goal. ***Seeing the value is the goal.*** Even if they see the value, not everyone can or will buy. Some will, though.

That's a game I enjoy playing. I love that kind of puzzle.

The "buy my book" constant promotion puzzle is exhausting, but the thought exercise of building the conditions as such so that people see the value is a fun game for me.

If you can shift that mindset, people who don't buy aren't rejecting you. They simply haven't met the conditions necessary to buy.

Even people who buy your other work have conditions to buy your future work. It's incumbent upon us to develop a strategy to meet those conditions.

But the money isn't the point. ***The connection is the point.***

If we don't make that connection between the buyer and the product, it is a failure of our marketing, not our work.

This is why it's so important to make a case for your book in many different ways. Most people have multiple conditions that must be met before they buy from you, even if they've bought from you before.

Some might be financial, but they might just as easily be about timing, connection, or any number of reasons.

Reframing your marketing through this lens allows you to stop seeing rejection as a personal attack and start seeing it as what it is…a chance to earn somebody's trust.

Yes, it is sad to find out somebody doesn't trust you yet, but you *can* earn trust. Once people trust you to write great books, they often will buy from you…

…if the conditions are right.

One of my favorite marketing reframes I've developed over the years is called "the theory of the case" or "the case for your book", depending on how I'm feeling that day.

The idea is that any marketing campaign is not about flashy graphics or slick copy but a concerted effort to make a case for why somebody should care about your book.

This isn't about begging, pleading, or cajoling but about looking at the positive reasons somebody should care about your book and overcoming the negative objections somebody might have.

During the Kickstarter campaign for Ichabod Jones: Monster Hunter volume 4, I broke this into six phases:

- **Initial announcement**—*0-28 days prior to launch*—From a month before launch until the day of launch, my job was to announce the book, reintroduce people to the series, and build excitement for the next volume so the launch goes well.
- **Launch**—*1-5 days after launch*—Once the book is launched, the next phase kicks into gear, and my job

is to capitalize on all the hype I have built up before launch. These are generally your traditional "ZOMG! It's live!" type outreach.

- **Sideways sales letter**—*5-12 days after launch*— Most writers are pretty okay up to here. They generally don't do nearly enough initial announcement outreach, but they usually send emails, but this is where their outreach stops. Mine, on the other hand, is just beginning. The sideways sales letter is a strategy where you break up your sales page, Kickstarter page, or other marketing across multiple emails. A sales page contains all the information a buyer needs in one place, but most people never read it, so instead I cut up the sales page and use it as outreach over several emails. You would not believe how many people read the page but miss some fact that causes them to buy.
- **Praise**—*14-21 days after launch*—Many of my launches don't go long enough to incorporate these other phases, but the next step I use when appropriate is to pull together reviews, email blurbs, and other nice things other people have said to show how much other people like me and/or my work.
- **Objection handling**—*22-28 days after launch*— Once I have talked about how much people like my work, my last phase before closing out a campaign is to take all the objections people have given me over the years and try to overcome them. For instance, many people have told me they don't read that series because they don't read horror, but Ichabod is more a fantasy book than anything. So, I state the objection and then overcome it.
- **Final countdown**—*29-31 days after launch*—If you have an evergreen launch model, where you're not doing time-based launches, then this doesn't fit, but one of the best ways to push people over the

edge is by using scarcity and telling people your offer is going to end. Even if you have an evergreen model, you can do things like pledge drives or limited-time offers to drive sales. I know many authors offer bonuses to people who buy during their pre-order period and upload proof of purchase to their website, for instance.

In each of these phases, you are shifting the narrative to make a case for your book to people who need more information to be convinced. One of my iron-clad marketing rules is that once somebody has seen a piece of marketing and decided not to buy, they will never buy from it.

That doesn't mean they will never buy, though, which is why you need a bunch of different pieces of marketing to build a case and persuade people to buy in other ways.

This also extends to your overall positioning in the market.

Since I am very into author ecosystems, I often think about how writers position themselves and their work to stand out from other writers and fit into the existing conversation.

This means not only asking yourself questions like "What is your point of view?" but also things like "Given my ideal reader has already read these things, how can I give a different perspective that builds and expands on but still fits with what has come before and what is going on right now".

Understanding that your audience also reads other things and is influenced by other things, so you have to position yourself relationally to them while offering your perspective, is one of the most important things for me.

Most writers seem to hate newsletters (*if they hate newsletters*) because they don't want to be a bother. They think of their email sends as the worst kind of "spam" that comes into their inboxes...

...but what if those emails were somebody's favorite thing to read every week?

Those supermarket coupons? Somebody has been waiting all week to see them.

Those blow-out sales? Somebody has been sitting on those to buy something they love.

Those Nigerian princes? Well, no. They are actually scam emails and annoying. However, even those emails usually allow somebody very lonely to be seen in a way they probably haven't in a long time.

Whatever way you slice it, people wouldn't send emails if nobody was excited to get them. You can bet that all around the world, lots of people are over the moon to save 64 cents on Campbell's Soup next week.

What if, instead of thinking of your emails as spam, you saw them for what they are...somebody's favorite email waiting to be found, the one they have been waiting for all week?

You might say, "That's impossible. I'm just sending an email about my new book launch," but I can assure you, if you've built your list correctly, your email will make somebody's day.

I am constantly shocked by how often people thank me for sending promotional emails to them. I get my share of bitterness, too, but I get way more support than I ever thought possible when I was starting.

In my main email automation sequence, I allow people to choose how often they hear from me. I tell them flat out that if they don't choose either weekly or monthly, they are giving me carte blanche to email them as often as I want, even multiple times a day.

The option to choose is at the bottom of every email I have sent for years, and still, less than 5% of people have chosen to hear from me unlimited times.

95% of people on my list are happy to hear from me as often as I want to send emails. *That's bonkers*. I've pulled back my email sends a lot over the years, but I used to send gobs of emails. Sometimes, during launches, I would email up to 4 times a day…and still almost nobody unsubscribed.

Yes, people do unsubscribe, yet most people don't. It's still wild to me, *but the truth is that some people want to hear from you.* To some people, you will be their favorite email.

If you move through the world with that truth, it will attract even more people to you.

Yes, some people might hate it, but those aren't your people. If you can focus on finding your people, this whole game becomes much easier.

All we're trying to do here, in all of this work, is find the people who resonate with what we do.

They are few and far between, but those moments you come across are magic.

I've gathered almost 200,000 emails over the years to find 20,000 or so that resonate with what I do and 5,000+ that have paid for it.

That's a fractional share of the number of people I've met in my career, but when you do this work for long enough and with intention, you can end up amassing a rather large group of humans who care about your work.

Some people have resonated with me for years, and others have only resonated with my work for a season.

It's always sad when somebody stops resonating with my work, but I try to take solace in the fact that it's magic to find anyone who resonates with me for even one second. This whole thing has nothing to do with money. It's all about resonance. ***Money is the byproduct of running a connection-focused business***, not the focus of it.

That doesn't mean we don't offer products and services to our audiences; it is quite the opposite.

Money comes because you have infused that connection into every bit of your work, and people want to support you for taking that much care with their attention.

If you treat that connection as a burden, either for you or for them, then you turn it into something bitter and ugly, but if you cherish it for the magic it is, then magic will flow through you.

Any good sales process is a discussion with your readers.

Writers love to talk about "engagement", but they tend to be haphazard and unintentional with their engagement regarding sales. Not to mention that social media engagement is a terrible way to judge buyer intention.

Not that engagement isn't important. Even if it doesn't lead to sales, the biggest reason many authors write is to connect with their readers. My point is that if we get good at asking readers what they want and then give it to them, the whole process becomes a lot easier.

I'm not necessarily talking about sharing the behind-the-scenes process of your work, but instead using that connection to ask direct questions like, "Why didn't you buy?" This is not meant to be an accusation or to make somebody feel guilty, but because I want to improve for next time.

After all, I am making this for them to enjoy. If they don't like it, I need to know why, not to shame them, but to give them what they want.

Conversely, when somebody does buy, it's important to ask, "Why did this resonate? What was different about this book?" Again, this isn't to be self-deprecating but to gain insight that will help improve the next book.

Nobody ever gets it perfect the first time, but you can't get the next one right if you don't know what you did and didn't get right this time.

Writers are hesitant to ask readers what they actually want to know, but the answers I got were life-changing, and people were all too happy to give me their opinions.

For instance, back in 2016, I was launching a lot of books that weren't connecting with readers. Since I was doing a lot of conventions at a time, I started to ask my fans what about my work wasn't working for them.

That year, I released a mystery novel, a children's book, and a YA novel…***none of which my fans wanted.***

What did they want? **Comics about monsters.** My two best-selling books at the time were *Ichabod Jones: Monster Hunter* and *Katrina Hates the Dead.*

I was building a comic book audience, and I wasn't giving them any comics!

The overwhelming response caused me to put *Monsters and Other Scary Shit*, a monster anthology, into production, which became my breakout hit.

Plus, when I launched that book, the marketing was easy because my audience told me what they wanted. I was giving it to them.

That doesn't mean I only give people what they want. After all, a big part of building a sustainable business is hearing what fans say and deciphering what they really mean.

Additionally, I write a lot of novels, so I had to do a lot of work convincing my audience they wanted prose books even though they never said they did. However, in general, my sales process involves using my engagement with readers to figure out what fans really want and then delivering that experience to them.

A ton of my marketing involves phrases like "Look at what I made for you" and "You told me this is what you wanted".

If you're having trouble embracing the sales process, then a really helpful reframe is to stop writing only what you want and start a conversation with your readers about what they want.

Then, deliver it to them.

If they still don't buy, then you need to:

- Ask better questions and/or
- Become a better translator between what your readers say and what they mean.

I have found that most problems arise because people don't spend enough time with customers to become great translators.

You can't learn how to translate English to French well without a lot of practice. Yes, you can be passable pretty quickly, but if you want to be world-class, you have to spend years learning the language until you can speak it without even thinking.

The same thing with learning to speak the language of your customers. Most people send maybe one survey a year and then talk to their fans in platitudes, never about anything that really matters.

If you're struggling with it, you probably need more reps to translate customer speak into what they really want.

What is it they say? "If a reader tells you something is wrong, they are always right. If they tell you how to fix it, they are always wrong."

If you ask more questions/ask better questions to more and more people, you will get better at it. *We grow where we put our focus.*

This doesn't mean stop writing the stories you love. It means finding the intersectionality between what readers want and what you love writing.

Using the conversation you're probably already having with your readers as a way to make your work resonate deeper with readers helps short-circuit the part of your brain that doesn't like sales…because you really aren't selling.

You're serving.

What does it mean to be "of service"?

Lots of people talk about being of service to their community, but they miss one crucial point. Being of service means engaging with a community without the expectation of reciprocation. I see so many people seeking to serve to get more followers, make more money, or boost their egos.

Those people often wonder loudly why they don't get anywhere…and it almost always flows back to those words.

You expect something.

That is not being of service to your community. It's counterintuitive, but good things happen when you do things without expectations.

The easiest way to get results is to stop doing things expecting results and to do them to be of service. Share insights without expectation of anything in return.

A huge part of being "of service" is to do things *without expectation of reciprocity.*

However, there is nothing that says people *can't* reciprocate, just that you *can't expect* them to reciprocate.

You can (***and should***) design your service to facilitate reciprocity, even if it's not given.

The difference is that I never expect people to buy anything I make. I made it because I thought people would like it.

I use my decades of experience to design products that I believe will resonate deeply with my ideal audience and then hope that resonance makes them want to buy it.

If they can't buy it for some reason, that's okay, but I know if I infuse my work with enough love and share it with the right people, some of them will buy it.

If you build a big enough audience, then those few souls who resonate deeply enough to buy are enough to make a decent living.

If you want to get better at sales and marketing, the single best reframe I have ever heard is this:

*Nobody buys because of you. They buy because of how **you** make **them** feel.*

They do not buy your memoir for your story. They buy it for how it can inform their story.

They don't buy your course because they love the platform you teach. They buy it because of the transformation you promise.

They don't buy your novel because of your name. They buy it for the promise your name delivers to them.

It's not always the most fun thing to think about, but none of this is about us. It's all about being of service to other people.

If you want more people to buy your books, you must focus not on what you teach but on what transformation, or universal fantasy, you hope to elicit in your readers.

If you think about your work this way, then pricing becomes a bit easier because you're not even selling the work. You're selling the transformation. The bigger the cost, the bigger the transformation you promise with your work.

It's as hard and as simple as that. The same is true with marketing. Lots of people get grossed out by marketing, but if you think of asking and receiving like a goodwill bank, it becomes easier.

You will ask for a lot from your audience when launching a product. They will be bombarded by it on every social media channel imaginable; you will be disseminating information dozens of times a day on multiple outlets. God help the people who follow you on multiple channels. They're the real heroes.

With so many updates about your product, it's easy for people to become annoyed with you and tired of your product. They will want to unsubscribe from your newsletter and unfollow you on social media. By the time your launch is over, they won't want to hear from you ever again.

The only way to combat this is to have a great relationship with your audience before you launch your product because you will torch it once your launch begins.

That's why you need to make deposits into the goodwill bank far in advance of any product launch. This is the crux of the value-first mentality. This is the business reason why we have to provide information to our audience and grow their trust before we ask for anything in return.

Because we will ask for something in return when we launch a product, and we will ask a lot. We will ask so much that any rational person will tune us out. But emotions aren't rational. People allow those they like and trust to get away with irrational things, like pounding them with reasons to buy their product.

That's why we need to build up massive goodwill before we even consider launching our product.

Think about your goodwill like it's a bank. We'll call it The First Bank of Goodwill. This bank works like any other bank, except that it runs on your goodwill instead of money.

When you do something nice for somebody, you deposit into this bank. Whether it's writing a blog post, speaking on a panel, providing advice over coffee, or even retweeting an interesting article, everything you do for your audience is a deposit in the goodwill bank.

By contrast, everything you ask of your audience is a withdrawal from the goodwill bank. Every time you ask somebody to buy your product, every time you pitch them something, and every single time you ask them to share your posts, you are withdrawing from your goodwill account.

If you have been depositing into the goodwill bank over and over again, you can make these withdrawals without over-drafting your account; however, if you haven't been making these deposits, then you can't afford to make an ask of your audience. Imagine trying to buy a $50,000 boat in cash when your checking account only has $3.27 in it. You just can't do that.

The same is true with your goodwill.

If you keep withdrawing from the goodwill bank without making deposits, there will be nothing left in your account when you need it. Without enough goodwill, your product launch won't be successful because your audience has no reason to support you. If you keep making those deposits, then you will always have enough goodwill in your account to sustain your withdrawals.

This is where most people screw up when it comes to launching a product. They haven't spent enough time making deposits into the goodwill bank to sustain their withdrawals, so their ask comes across as begging. It's perceived as brash and creates an uncomfortable situation. Instead of people gladly buying the product, they either bristle at the thought of buying or only buy out of pity. This type of customer doesn't stick around for the long haul.

This is why making deposits into the goodwill bank is such an important concept. If you do it correctly, you'll always have a massive amount of goodwill available when it's time to launch your product. With that goodwill built up, your audience will gladly buy from you instead of recoiling from your ask.

Just note that making deposits into the goodwill bank is a perpetual task you must perform throughout your career. You can't just use it on your first launch and coast on the interest forever. Your goodwill account is like a checking account—it doesn't build interest.

Luckily, goodwill is easy to deposit if you are a good person who wants to serve your audience. If you come from a place of service and value, then almost everything you do will make a deposit into the goodwill bank.

A simple formula I use is to give more than I ask. If I ask a lot, then I have to give a lot.

However, it's important to remember that people want to support you making more they can enjoy. You are helping them. Yes, there is an exchange of money, but if you fill your audience with the right people, you are serving them by making things, and by buying your work, they are helping you make more things for them.

I work hard to develop a different paradigm with my readers than one that relies on capitalism, but usually, truth be told, it does depend on capitalism. I hire artists, editors, admins, and other contract staff and then leverage their work to obtain a greater value than I paid in the market.

That's capitalism, and I don't love it. I try to make myself feel better by saying that I'm helping pay their bills and survive, but on some level, I know that is just a platitude that capitalists say to feel better about themselves.

I've talked about turning my company into an autonomous collective for years, but I am pragmatic enough to recognize when I'm lying to myself.

Part of doing this work is realizing that you are probably not the noble paragon of virtue you think you are, especially if you want to make money from your writing. The more you want to scale your author business, the more compromises you must make with yourself.

Hopefully, you can find some balance in it so you don't sell your whole soul even as you piecemeal it out over your career.

That is not a very cheery thought, but it is the truth. You absolutely can make a living as an artist, but the question becomes how much you can compromise without losing yourself in the process.

Just remember, no matter how much capitalism tries to tie your worth to the amount of money you generate to feed it, you have intrinsic self-worth just for being alive.

You are worthy of being alive simply by being alive. You don't have to make or do something to be worthy of that. You have as much value and worth as kings, CEOs, and the homeless.

It has been the work of a lifetime to understand that my self-worth is not coupled with my success. It's not tied to my productivity.

WHAT CHRONIC ILLNESS CAN TEACH US ABOUT CONSERVING OUR ENERGY FOR WHAT MATTERS AND TAKING IMPERFECT ACTION

I have been chronically ill for 20 years. It started with mono back in college and then cascaded to hyperthyroidism, then stomach issues, and then migraines…

…come to think of it, I had migraines when I was 12, so maybe it's close to 30 years, but those migraines cleared up until recently, so I really don't count it as an unbroken chain…

…although that also doesn't take into account the anxiety and depression I've had for as far back as I can remember.

Long story short, I've been sick for a while. There has been a (mostly) unbroken chain of chronic illness for two decades. Some of my chronic illnesses are nearly old enough to drink.

They tend to compete with each other for supremacy, and I feel very much like Mr. Burns in that classic episode of The Simpsons, where he finds out he has every illness.

I won't say that chronic illnesses are a good thing by any stretch, but they do put things into perspective, especially when stuff goes wrong.

There is nothing that will stop my chronic illnesses. I can allay them for a time, but they will always flare up because they are chronic, which is what that word means.

Even if all my illnesses went into remission for the rest of my life tomorrow, there will still be the ever-present fear in the back of my brain, wondering when the time bomb will go off again.

Still, there *are* good things about them.

For instance, I stopped asking why random things happened because I knew the truth; there is really no logical reason. Some things just happen.

Bad things happen to good people.

Good things happen to good people.

Mostly, things happen randomly and without reason. As a person who grew up believing he could reason his way out of most things, succumbing to the whims of an uncaring universe helps me get through every single day.

Without that knowledge, I would be insufferable…well, more insufferable.

The world is chaotic, but there is beauty in that chaos. It took a long time, but I learned it is often enough to know *that*, even if you don't know *why*.

In March of 2023, I lost my Facebook account. I don't know exactly *why* it happened or *why* it happened then, but

I know *that* it happened, and those facts allow me to move on and do what I have to do to survive.

If I tried to dissect every random slight and incongruity, I would descend into madness. It is only by succumbing to the chaos that I can move on and see the good in the bad.

Seeing the good in the bad is essential to getting through life with a chronic illness, and if you look hard enough, the bad can help you see things you couldn't otherwise.

My dog doesn't like to eat dinner sometimes. *We don't know why.* All his tests came out normal, but he's had a hard life. He was brought over from China after being saved from a dog meat factory and has a huge bald spot on his neck from having tufts of hair ripped out.

Still, he's a happy (if often aloof) boy, but sometimes he doesn't like to eat. Maybe it's trauma. Maybe he has an undiagnosed condition. Maybe he's just picky.

It doesn't really matter *why*. It matters *that*.

Usually, we bring him into another room or follow him around the house until he finally eats (because our other dog will goblin it up if we leave it out).

Don't be taken in by her cuteness. This little dog is a bottomless pit for food.

Since Cocoa (*our bigger dog*) gets so much more food than Cheyenne (*our smaller dog*), we can't just leave it out. So, sometimes, it becomes quite the show.

Earlier this week, however, my splitting headache prevented me from doing anything but setting the bowl down in our bedroom and closing the door so Cheyenne couldn't get at the food.

I didn't push the food on him. I simply sat and petted him for a while. Eventually, he chose to eat on his own, and that was beautiful.

I felt like we had a breakthrough that would never have happened if I had arrogantly pushed my will on my poor dog.

Why didn't he eat? I don't know.

I knew ***that*** he didn't eat, though, and being okay with that allowed me to get him to eat and allowed him to survive another day until we can figure out the deeper why.

But also…there might not be one. There might not be a ***why***, only a ***that***.

Survival is important to somebody with chronic illnesses. Why did you wake up so tired that you can barely move? Which of your chronic illnesses is dragging you down today? Why can't you eat a certain food now that you could for years without your body falling apart?

After years and years, it matters less ***why*** one of my ailments is flaring up and it matters more ***that*** it is flaring up because it is only in accepting it is happening that allows me to relieve the problem, mitigate the damage, and prevent it from happening again.

Chronic illness is all about mitigating damages, and to do that, you must be constantly analyzing yourself for signs of distress.

I'm always analyzing my launches to figure out how to do them better and how to help people better in the future.

But, when you are in the middle of a failing launch, it doesn't much matter *why* things are happening, at least not nearly as much as knowing *that* it is happening and what you can do to mitigate the damage.

Once you have done that, you can analyze why it happened at a deeper level and try to prevent it from happening again, but *you have to take action now to survive.*

I use the word *try* very deliberately because you cannot guarantee that your problem will never happen again, and sometimes the thing that saved you one day will destroy you the next.

I used to swear by melatonin to sleep. Then, one night, it started giving me migraines so bad I couldn't do anything the next day. I have no idea *why*, but I know *that* I stopped using it, and the migraines stopped. I don't sleep anymore, which is a far cry better than writhing in agony.

It was important to know why I had a migraine, but why did something that helped me for so long turn on me suddenly? *I can't care about that part.* Some doctors try to answer those questions, but they almost always say, "Don't do that, then".

It is not a perfect solution, but *there are no perfect solutions*. That's kind of the point of chronic illnesses. You will never be perfect again, and if you want to do more than survive, you have to be okay with not being okay.

When you are in the thick of it, barely able to get through the day, knowing *that* will often save you *in the moment,* while knowing *why* will fix the underlying issue, if there is anything to fix.

Which is something else I learned.

There is often no fix.

There is merely a workaround you hope works long-term. Sometimes it does, and sometimes it doesn't.

Did square ads work last month? Cool. Maybe they will work again this month. Maybe something else will work tomorrow.

Maybe you'll be running along just fine for years, and suddenly, Facebook will flag your account twice in a month even though nothing has changed and you have violated none of their rules.

I'm not saying you don't need to know why, but *why* often stifles fixing *that* which is threatening to destroy us *right now* until we can figure out the deeper why.

I would be dead if I didn't know why my thyroid levels were off back when I was 28. They put me on medication, which worked for a decade, and it saved my life.

It was a ticking time bomb, though.

Eventually, those thyroid drugs stopped working. Why did they stop working that day at that time? No idea. We always knew that one day, they might stop working, but there was no way to determine when that might happen.

When they did, it didn't matter *why*. It mattered *that*.

After they stopped working, I had to get radiation on that thyroid, which killed it for good, but not before my thyroid tried to kill me one last time.

I didn't know *why* I almost died that night last February and not any of the days before or since, but I sure knew *that* I was dying, which saved my life.

The why was critically important to my care, but it didn't help much in my day-to-day life. Able-bodied people think knowing why your body stopped working correctly leads to a miracle where you never feel bad again…

…but that's not the case.

Once you have your treatment plan, most of dealing with chronic illnesses is pain management and knowing what triggers you.

Knowing that you are in pain allows you to take action to mitigate that pain.

Managing an author business is a lot like having a chronic illness. You're constantly looking for signs of distress and making sure you are able to survive from one day to the next.

You test, and you plan. You eat healthily, and you exercise to keep the beating heart of your business healthy, but most of the time, you're trying not to kill it…

…and often, it's about knowing *that* certain things trigger flare-ups, even if you can't pin down *why*.

If you go through your business life wondering why things happened to you and lamenting that it's not fair, you're missing the point.

None of this is fair. Good or bad, there is always a bit of randomness in everything. Your book is probably just as good as more popular books in your genre, and the only reason it's not being read by more people is bad luck.

There is great luck in authorship, but there is also almost always a parasite threatening your business and trying to kill it off.

When you get sick, you have to control the fever first…because the fever can kill you just as easily, or more easily, than the parasite.

Lots of people die around the world because their body, while trying to fight the infection, creates internal conditions that kill them.

If you keep asking why ***without taking action***, then you'll fail to keep your business alive, and by the time you turn your attention to dealing with the ***that***, you'll have disrupted the ecosystem irreparably before you even have time to unearth the ***why***.

But more importantly, ***there usually is no why,*** except that the universe is chaotic, and we can only ever impose so much order into the system.

Why did a long-time reader stop reading? Maybe there is a problem you can fix, but often, the best answer is just…because it happened. Even if you do everything perfectly, 2-5% of your readers will churn every year, many through no fault of your own.

Knowing that fact, if you want to grow, you need to find at least 5% more readers every year, or you will shrink. Knowing ***that***, you can take some action, even if you don't know ***why***.

It might not be a perfect action, but *it is often the imperfect action that saves your life or alleviates your suffering so you can try again tomorrow.*

That is why you need to create multiple paths for success and have direct access to the most fans possible. It's why you need to be set up on as many platforms as possible. It's why you need the most control possible.

Once you fix the thing trying to kill you, then you can look at the situation and build better systems. The better your systems, the less risk you have day-to-day.

The cleaner your water, the fewer parasites you will have trying to kill you. Still, you can't change the entire water system of your city at once, but you can boil water to save your health and your life right now.

It's an imperfect solution *that* will save your life today and allow you to deal with the deeper *why* tomorrow when you aren't doubled over in pain.

The more redundancy we can build into our business, the less any one failure point can cripple us, and the more chances we have to catch the things *that* do go wrong, even if we don't know *why* they go wrong.

Chronic illnesses are all about creating systems of protection to insulate you from those things that will throw you into a spiral. It's about surrounding yourself with the things that will allow you to thrive and prevent your own body from trying to kill you.

I won't lie. I had a nervous breakdown when Facebook deleted my account. I don't mean that metaphorically. I meant I was sitting in front of my computer, babbling incoherently and crying because I thought everything was over.

It was horrible, and I felt my whole body crumbling under me. I don't think I have ever felt that so acutely in my entire life.

My wife, in her infinite wisdom, somehow convinced me to go to bed, and the next morning, I woke up with a fresh outlook…

…maybe it wasn't so bad.

I owned the buyer data for most of my customers and collected emails on my website. It's the most important part of my business, outside of writing books. If I couldn't connect with them, it would destroy everything tomorrow.

I have contingencies upon contingencies built into my businesses. I insist on it, and while I often feel like a crazy person, I am also living proof that something is always out there trying to kill you.

You can keep your business healthy by maintaining a safe distance from the things you know are trying to kill you and creating systems with multiple redundancy layers so that when systems fail, and they will, your business doesn't collapse in on itself.

As authors, we need to create an ecosystem that is robust, but there will always be randomness to it, and that randomness can kill your mental health if you can't come to terms with the fact that the *why* might never be known, but you can always deal with the *that*.

I don't know why my girlfriend cheated on me all those years ago and gave me mono, which threw my whole body into chaos, but I do know that it happened, and I know even better that there is no *why* to solve. There is only a *that* to manage.

I never talked to her again after she told me what she did, but I don't resent her for it. ***Resentment is for healthy people***. I don't have time to wallow in *why* I was so unlucky because if I resented one thing, I would end up resenting everything.

Instead, I get up and put one foot in front of the other, trying to make the best of the *that* which I have been given. These days, when I think of her in fleeting moments of memories long past, it is mostly to hope she has not suffered the same way I have for all these years.

If you had told me all those years ago that one moment would define my whole life, I would have laughed in your face. And yet, here I am.

Maybe you find that depressing, but there is great freedom in that for me because, for the most part, I can let the *why* float down the river out of sight and deal with the matter of *that* which keeps me alive to live another day.

HOW TO FALL IN LOVE WITH BOOK MARKETING

I have been listening to Kesha's music since she was making trashy club songs , and I was a trash panda getting wasted in bars every weekend. Her work provided the theme of my early adulthood.

She transformed her career into deeper, more soulful music at a time when all my bar friends moved away, and I started to contemplate my life more deeply. While the legal case surrounding her lawsuit broke my heart, her fight to control her career, her IP, and her life resonated deeply with me as a creator trying to understand the pitfalls of massive success.

After not being able to release an album for years, the records that finally came out were some of the best I've ever heard in my life. I have big feelings about whether you must be sad to create great art. However, there is no doubt accessing that trauma allowed Kesha to create transformative music on a deeper level than in her early career. Of course, she could have made this music from the beginning if she hadn't been micromanaged and sexually abused by her producer.

Suffice it to say, I am a big fan of Kesha's work from way back in the Ke$ha days and feel deeply connected to her work on a spiritual level I reserve for very few people.

However, I am not a member of any online community for her work, and I don't post about her music often. I have a few friends who geek out with me when a new song drops, and I get very, very excited every time she sends an email (*which is only a few times a year*). As far as I know, she doesn't host a Reddit or manage a Facebook group, and she's not focused on connecting members of her fandom in the way we are normally taught how to do it.

I would pay an ungodly sum of money to watch Kesha read the phone book, and yet, by the parlance of how we talk about community, Kesha is awful at fostering a connection to and community around her work.

That can't be possible because literally millions upon millions of people care about her music and feel deeply connected to her struggle…

…which means that maybe, just maybe, everything we know about building community in specific and building a creative business, in general, is built on a web of half-truths and faulty logic.

I've talked about "the stack" for years, pulling the idea from web development and marketing tech. The idea was that every industry has a "stack" that they are taught to be successful. To be a "full stack developer", you need to learn it all.

- *For indie book publishing,* authors are taught writing to market, book packaging, Amazon ads, Facebook ads, and newsletter management, among others.

- ***For creating comics,*** you learn how to create a book that looks amazing, Kickstarter, social media community building, and convention sales, among others.
- ***For non-fiction,*** you learn how to explain the scope of an opportunity, create courses, build sales funnels, release weekly content, and speak in front of a crowd, among other things.
- ***For journalism,*** you're taught the upside-down triangle, creating newsworthy content that gets people to stay on-site longer, and how to retain readers through subscriptions.

This is an oversimplification of the success strategies taught in each area of publishing I've worked in throughout my life, but if you squat in any forum about these topics for long enough, a "stack" of important principles starts to emerge that unites the community in a collective shorthand. It is the shared language we all use to communicate and identify others "in the know".

It is amazing to have that kind of shorthand, but it also creates a problematic culture that stifles innovation. When you spend too much in a specific community, people start to think that their way is the only way and begin to lash out at other concepts that don't fit perfectly inside their neatly constructed model of success, fostering a culture riddled with survivorship bias that suffers from groupthink on a systemic level.

I have talked about authors using Kickstarter, for instance, since at least 2015, but was roundly told it could never work. Meanwhile, I was earning a profit on very niche books in an industry where almost nobody breaks even. It wasn't until Brandon Sanderson raised $41 million on

Kickstarter that authors widely started to accept that Kickstarter might be a good idea.

Then, in short order, it became part of "the indie author stack". Huge swaths of authors started incorporating it into their businesses…and things quickly went to pot as many authors found it wasn't the gold rush they had been promised.

To be fair, by and large, authors have found tons of success on Kickstarter. Authors and publishers in our Kickstarter Accelerator course have raised close to $1.5 million for their projects, and we've changed countless more lives through our books. Still, it turns out that Kickstarter is not a magic bullet that suddenly fixes a broken system for everyone.

I admit my part in saying that all authors should use Kickstarter, but it quickly became apparent in the past year that while some people will crush it on Kickstarter, others will fizzle out, and even some seven-figure authors won't be able to raise $500 on it.

But why, though? Why is it a platform that literally changes the course of one author's life and completely blows up in another's face? Why is it that even if you account for follower count, mailing list size, income, and effort, and you find two authors who study the same system and implement it in roughly the same way, their success on Kickstarter will vary wildly? *And why didn't I see it until it unfolded in front of my face?*

I can't be 100% sure about that last part, but it seems clear I was so focused on both my own success and the survivorship bias of those who crushed it on Kickstarter that I failed to understand a simple truth staring me right in the face…*some people are better suited to how the Kickstarter launch cycles work than others*.

It turns out that before the Brandon Sanderson campaign, for the most part, the people who used Kickstarter were the ones who already wanted to integrate it into their businesses, which propped up the success metrics for everyone. *When everyone started using it, whether they saw it as a good fit or not, more people realized that it didn't work for them.*

We still have almost a 100% success rate among our students, but a pattern of failure started to emerge, and we fell down the rabbit hole, looking into what caused it for months.

I've been trying to build a community for years in the ways that "gurus" tell you to build communities. I've tried Facebook, Discord, and Circle, but nothing worked. I have applied hundreds of strategies to boost engagement, but none of them worked, either.

Meanwhile, I have a mailing list of 20,000+ people with an open rate above 40%. Even when I send daily during a marketing campaign, *people still open and read*.

On top of that, when I launch a new book, people get excited to buy it. We launched a Circle community earlier this year to try yet again to build a community. While it was failing spectacularly, I successfully launched four projects and a conference, *making over $100,000 while my community died a wordless death.*

So, it's not like I have a dead list of people who don't care. *My fans care deeply.* They just don't engage with each other much in a community setting. On top of that, it's not how I'm wired. I am particularly bad at fostering that kind of engagement…

…but that's the only way we're told a community can exist.

So, if a community is critical to success, and you can only build one if you foster engagement across the community, then *why is my community thriving even though we almost never engage with each other?*

It turns out "the stack" we're force-fed about building a community is completely wrong, and there are actually many ways to build a community around your work that aren't talked about at all.

The more I searched for community-building advice from outside my normal sources, the less broken I felt. Meanwhile, dogmatic adherence to "the stack" made me feel like a failure. *While "the stack" acts as a shorthand to socialize members of a community, it also isolates them from new ideas.* At its worst, teaching "the stack" actually destroys as many, or more, careers than it helps create by telling people there is only one way to do things.

Seth Godin says culture is about showing your community that "people like us do things like this", but it turns out, like most things, the truth falls into a murky gray area not easily explored through ironic tweets and pithy comments.

I don't even blame the experts. A culture quickly calcifies around certain ideas and rewards people who talk about those ideas in ways that reinforce the monolith of "the stack". As I found out first-hand, it takes an incredible amount of effort to push that monolith even a fraction of an inch, and all the while, the industry will do its best to return to the mean.

Because of my myriad chronic illnesses, I've spent a lot of time in doctor's offices over the past 20 years, and I've been with Kaiser for the better part of a decade. If you come from a country with a functional medical system, then Kaiser is the closest analog I've found to the NHS in all the best and worst ways.

Kaiser is excellent at dealing with known medical problems. If your illness falls in the middle of the Bell Curve, then they can handle you with smashing success. If, however, you have an illness that presents differently than the norm, or if you have an illness that is not easily diagnosable, then the whole system breaks down.

As such, I've had to spend a lot of time with personalized medicine over the past few years trying to find ways to live inside this body, and what I've found is fascinating.

Did you know, for instance, that the same foods can cause different glucose reactions in different people? My wife and I could eat the same amount of food at the same time and have very different reactions depending on how our bodies process it.

Or, did you know that the order in which you eat food matters? If certain people eat nuts before they eat fruit, they can cut off the glucose spike that comes from sugary food.

Or that for some people, ice cream is better than fruit because of the high levels of fat?

I could go on forever, but the point is that while there is a "stack" of medical knowledge that is broadly applicable to many people, in almost every case, you should be personalizing the results for your own body.

Additionally, just because something works for one person in a certain way, chances are it will work differently for you if it works at all.

This is where experts and gurus can help. They can give us a broad scope of opportunities and best practices to solve a problem. They also can diagnose an issue and tell us what not to do to prevent catastrophic failure.

I had to get my thyroid irradiated last year, and while the process almost killed me, I was sure happy the doctors could properly diagnose the problem, fix it, and put me on the right pills to manage it.

They got me 90% of the way there, but now it's on me to find the right balance to make my life liveable.

Other patients might need way more personalization in their lives. For instance, we know frighteningly little about most conditions, like Chronic Fatigue Syndrome. Medical science can do almost nothing to help people with CFS right now. Doctors can help give some direction, but it's 95% on patients to find ways to make their lives not miserable.

I've watched personalized medicine completely change people's lives on both ends of the spectrum. We've now entered a world where a personalized "stack" is the way forward for authors.

Just like with personalized medicine, finding your personalized ecosystem will help some authors get that extra 5% to lock everything into place. For other authors, though, it could turn their unsuccessful business into a thriving one.

The rest of this chapter is a collaboration between Monica and me as we introduce the concept of Author Ecosystems to you.

After working with thousands of authors to help turn their love of writing and publishing into a sustainable career, ***we have observed five clear and unique publishing ecosystems (or archetypes) that closely align with author success.*** We believe that identifying your ideal author ecosystem and focusing on marketing actions that work with your natural tendencies is the surest path to thrive as an author.

We've mapped these archetypes onto the five ecosystem biomes on Earth (***Desert, Grassland, Tundra, Forest,*** and ***Aquatic***) to provide a clear, easily visualized metaphor for each type and linked them to successful publishing strategies that work best for each one. We've also identified healthy and unhealthy habits for each type and ***have developed guidance to create a healthy ecosystem and foster a sustainable author career using strategies that align with your natural strengths.***

While we've created this framework to work across the entire publishing cycle, including craft and mindset, our focus remains on sales and marketing, and this is where we think we can help people create individualized plans for themselves the most.

Some of the questions we hope the Author Ecosystem Archetypes can answer include:

- Why am I struggling to turn my writing into a career?
- What advice should I take (and what can I filter out)?

- How can I prevent burnout while building my career?

Depending on your archetype, there will be certain things that resonate with you more than others, and you should be able to pull things out of "the stack" that help you to thrive and abandon things that don't serve you.

I'll be talking about this a lot more moving forward as it's the direction we're taking all our teaching modalities, but as this is already a lot of information, for now, I want to introduce each of the five ecosystems and tell you a little bit about them.

DESERT

- **Most important resource:** arbitrage through optimization
- **Superpowers:** ability to spot trends before others, ease at producing books that readers are excited about, ability to make business decisions within writing the book
- **Natural aptitudes:** KU, webstore, advertising, capturing "virality"
- **Examples of Deserts:** Dan Brown, William Shakespeare, EL James, Suzanne Collins, Michael Anderle

Deserts are pliable creators who excel at writing to market and identifying hot trends that audiences want to read at any given moment. They can make unemotional business decisions and "ride a trend" by delivering on the hot tropes in the market before it vanishes. If you've ever met somebody who always seems to hit the right trends at the right time, they are probably a Desert.

Because Deserts are good at riding trends, they need to have a few different skill sets, including strong research skills, the ability to produce quickly, and a willingness to detach—both to double down on what's working well and to cut activity on anything that's not working. ***Deserts tend to put all their sustenance in one cactus and build a highly profitable pathway for readers to sales.***

Deserts tend to do great, for instance, in KU, because their superpower is being able to find what huge groups of people are searching for at any given time and deliver something those readers want while their frenetic energy is at its highest peak. This brings more money in the short-term, though it can put their business at risk if any aspect of their system—audience, money, or market forces—dries up. ***Many Deserts balance this risk by having multiple pen names or by maintaining a freelance career on the side that they can always fall back on in tough times.***

Successful Deserts thrive on writing to market and rapid-releasing books, but this doesn't work for any other ecosystem. A Desert's ability to detach from the material and write fast to trend without the need to infuse themselves into the text allows them to work faster with less mental drain than other ecosystems.

We estimate that a significant percentage of struggling KU authors are other ecosystems trying unsuccessfully to be Deserts. Unfortunately, since they either incorrectly judge upcoming trends, can't write fast enough to capitalize on trends without burning out, or infuse too much of themselves into their books to capitalize on trends, it does not work for them.

This is not helped by the fact that to be at the forefront of emerging niches it behooves Deserts to play their cards close to the vest and observe much more than they speak.

Healthy Deserts maintain a camel hump (or several) where they can store away their "riches in the niches" to sustain them between oases where water is plentiful. They watch the warning signs that the market is changing, and they pivot when necessary—to another genre, to another source of readers, or to another platform.

Unhealthy Deserts stray too far from a water source and end up thirsty when one or several of their money makers dries up. Additionally, they have a habit of "planting" a book and running away before that series can take root. Even though succulents can survive on very little maintenance, they do need to be watered well until they take root, while unhealthy Deserts are always on to the next trend.

Deserts do best when the arbitrage between how many books a category can support and how many books are in it is very high. If you've ever seen a K-lytics report, then you'll know that the best opportunities for Deserts often result in a "hot" genre before too many people know about it.

While other ecosystems can survive on little or no arbitrage (and even get a bump from a "mature genre", as we call it), Deserts survive by hopping from genre to genre, looking for the biggest arbitrage opportunities and creating new reader profiles for each one.

This leads to a back catalog that doesn't have a ton of value, as once the trend dies, they aren't sticking around to follow the author. This was a huge problem for pulp writers, some of whom wrote hundreds of books, making a good living without having any recognition or books that stood the test of time.

GRASSLAND

- **Most important resource:** focus and depth
- **Superpowers:** Good at spotting trends, repositioning themselves in the market, persisting on one area of focus, becoming above reproach, and creating the best of the best in the niche
- **Natural aptitudes:** Medium, Substack, fiction app, wide retailers
- **Examples of Grasslands:** Terry Pratchett, Cassandra Clare, George R.R. Martin, Monica Leonelle

Grasslands are focused, deep delvers who seek out popular topics that align with their interests. These are the industry thought leaders who correctly predict emerging trends and then become such experts that they literally know everything about them. Once they effectively "own" the topic, they get an outmoded benefit of both SEO and word of mouth that compounds over time.

These are the authors we follow to understand a complicated topic. Unlike Deserts, who are encouraged to keep their cards close to the vest to maximize a trend, a Grassland finds true value in explaining complex emerging trends to "own the space" and drawing attention to it so they reap the benefits of backlinks to their work and referrals from other professionals to fuel their growth.

Grasslands plant a lot of seeds to feel out a topic, but when they find something that takes root with a large potential audience, they quickly go extremely deep with it—deeper than anyone else has the energy to do. *If you always turn to the same person when you need to understand the nuance of a specific topic better, they are probably a Grassland.*

Grasslands tend to consider every angle of their genre, niche, or topic so that when they put something out, it tends to blow people's minds and rise to the top. *Like with Deserts, a key to Grassland's success is that they are right about the emerging trends that will captivate their audiences for years to come.*

A ton of authors we speak to think they are a Grassland, but no matter how much attention they give to a topic, the trend either never emerges or they don't "own the topic" when it does. *Being right and going deep are marketing tactics that Grasslands use to separate themselves from everyone else in the field.* Meanwhile, the sheer length of time they can talk about a topic prevents competition from emerging to challenge them.

Grasslands are capable of becoming the absolute best-in-class at whatever they do, which is why they need to choose new potential projects carefully.

Because Grasslands are intense and obsessive about their chosen topic, they must stay focused to see the fruits of it. It does not serve them well to have multiple projects going at once because they don't have the energy to devote to each one. It also doesn't typically work for them to cross over audiences between two different interests, unlike some of the other types.

Healthy Grasslands find fertile soil to take root in and grow the tallest, most epic tree in the garden. They also dedicate so much of their energy to one area that they become above reproach. Unhealthy Grasslands plant a lot of seeds but never gain momentum in any one area, struggle to deliver on deadlines they've set for themselves, or try to plant too many trees than their ecosystem can support.

One of the hardest things for Grasslands to do is consider something done and ready to be sold. They find it almost impossible to stop tweaking things, and even when they do, they have an even harder time saying, "Did you know you could buy this?" Grasslands have created incredible goodwill with their fans, but they need to get out of their own way and actually tell people about the things they can buy from them.

Grasslands will probably, and should probably, choose 1-2 topics and cover them for their entire careers. For a non-fiction author, that might mean choosing a field or a specialty within a field. In contrast, for a fiction author, it probably means writing a lot of books in one series, along with world-building books, spinoffs, and a whole lot of content that goes beyond even the books themselves.

TUNDRA

- **Most important resource:** Excitement
- **Superpowers:** Launching, getting people excited and pointing attention to themselves and their work
- **Natural aptitudes:** Kickstarter, landing pages, conventions, KU
- **Examples of Tundras:** Tim Ferriss, Sherrilyn Kenyon, Rick Riordan, Russell Nohelty, Melanie Harlow

Tundras love to build cool things and launch them, and they are extremely well-versed in turning a ton of attention to themselves and their project for a short period of time. They are the type to study a platform and see what trends they can tap into to make their next launch bigger, *and they are most likely to know how they are going to market and sell something before creating it.* Once done with a project, they wipe their hands free of it and rarely think much of it again—the launch is over!

Tundras are naturally able to understand the evergreen trends in a genre and stack them on top of each other in a way that gets people super excited. While a Desert focuses on current trends and leaps between them often, and a Grassland focuses on emerging trends they can sink their teeth into for years, Tundras generally focus on evergreen trends and find ways to use them in unique ways that will get everyone in their target market excited for a new launch.

Because Tundras survive on a feast and famine cycle, they need to be able to peel as much meat from the bone as possible. *Tundras become stackers—stackers of trend, stackers of value, stackers of audience.* They are comfortable with having many one-off projects and comfortable with building a diverse audience that only likes a portion of their catalog—though they welcome superfans who enjoy everything, too.

This is why Kickstarter is naturally perfect for Tundras— because we are launchers and know how to get a small, niche audience excited about something cool. While Kickstarter is also great for other ecosystems, Tundras are naturally wired to understand how to use it. While Deserts are great at riding trends and Grasslands have stickiness, *Tundras tend to have a preternatural ability to*

hit #1 in the Amazon store and use that excitement to keep their books selling.

Healthy Tundras have a firm understanding of their feast seasons and build safeguards to make sure there's never a point of starvation. They also learn to connect their body of work—usually somewhat disparate projects—under one banner so that every launch offers a bigger feast on their backlist. Unhealthy Tundras struggle to create enough feasts to get through the famine periods, leaving them burnt out and under-resourced before the next launch.

FOREST

- **Most important resource:** shared language and interconnectivity
- **Superpowers:** Injecting their personalities into their books, high competency and skill stacking, nurturing every project consistently
- **Natural tendencies:** Patreon, Ream, wide sales, live events
- **Examples of Successful Forests:** Stephen King, Brandon Sanderson, JK Rowling, Colleen Hoover

Forests march to the beat of their interests and put their unique spin on everything they do for their readers. They have a close relationship with their fans largely because they inject so much of their personality into all their books. They could write a murder mystery, a sweet romance, or a cozy comedy and readers will gobble it up because it's their unique take on a genre.

The biggest problem with Forests is they always think they are some other ecosystem. Forests really want to be "in on the party", so they act like Deserts, but they write too much of themselves in their books to maximize trends.

Forests also really like digging deep into their nerdy interests, so they think they are Grasslands, but when they try to share their interests, nobody cares outside their community.

Forests also like providing cool stuff for their audience, so they try to launch like Tundras, but they haven't stacked enough tropes to build excitement outside their community to get people talking.

When they focus on their superpower of building interconnectivity between all their work and finding people who grok their slant on the world, they thrive.

Because Forests are multi-passionate, they tend to have multiple pen names going at once. Whereas this might overwhelm other types, Forests are good at watering each of their trees on a consistent schedule so everything grows steadily. They are extremely competent and tend to stack an impressive number of skills to deliver high-quality work across everything they do. Forests are good at being top of the class and being part of the conversation.

To do this, Forests must be consistent, hard-working, and patient, as it takes time, energy, and money to stand up each of their trees (and they still need to do so one at a time to get a bit of momentum in one area before moving on to another). This is also the ecosystem that takes the longest to get momentum, so it's very important to have at least one standout series that can draw people in as you build your community. However, once they are rocking and rolling, there is usually no stopping them.

Healthy Forests survive by cross-pollinating their work across all their interests. The key connection is their personality, and their fans gravitate toward them for who they are rather than what they do or write. Unhealthy

Forests chase trends, focus too much on their existing community without bringing in enough new readers, and don't pay close enough attention to the marketplace to ensure enough readers will share their interests to draw them into their ecosystem.

Tying this back to their superpower, a Forest does not need to be the hub of their audience, unlike a Tundra or a Grassland, which is a common misnomer of this ecosystem. Instead, they need to help build a shared language among their fans so that they can talk with each other. The best Forests are able to create engagement between their fans without them even being there. The more you can do this, the more powerful your audience becomes.

AQUATIC

- **Most important resource:** Vision
- **Superpowers:** Huge vision, high energy, team building, brand management
- **Natural aptitudes:** Kickstarter, Patreon, Ream, live events, wide
- **Examples of Aquatics:** Stephenie Meyer, Stan Lee, George Lucas

Aquatics are excited about everything and want to create an immersive experience for their fans. They know exactly what their fans want, and this dictates both what they create and how they market it. If their fans want to see their bestselling novel as a comic book, they create it for them— even if they have no idea how to do a comic book.

The key with Aquatics is that they are brand managers. Their loyalty is to the overall brand and servicing their fans with different types of products. Aquatics see books as a means to service fans of their brand, but they are equally excited about RPGs, pins, movies, and everything else that can exist beyond the books.

Because Aquatics build their business to maximize customer lifetime value across an entire brand by leveraging many different formats, ***they must be competent at many skill sets,*** like building large stories and worlds, delegating responsibilities, building a functional team that understands the bigger vision, maintaining a strong connection to fans, and expanding slowly and as time, energy, money, and other resources allow.

Often, an Aquatic is intentionally overshadowed by the brand they are growing. Usually, your first introduction to an Aquatic is through one of the many tendrils they have extended, pointing back to their brand. Whereas a Forest is almost always central to their brand, an Aquatic often disappears into the background.

Healthy Aquatics thrive by creating cool new products that both service their current audience and help them grow a larger audience in different pockets of fandom. Unhealthy Aquatics create too many products without having a team in place to help share the load, spread themselves too thin and lose momentum by growing too fast, or create products they want to exist instead of focusing on what their audience wants to buy from them.

Because they tend to see inefficiencies and flaws in systems, they often create their own category by looping several of them together to create something new. Companies like Southwest and Apple are great examples of this, but also trends like Omegaverse and Romantasy on the fiction side. Because of the way Aquatics think, they create systems that can't be broken apart and used easily by others, which is how they win. Even 50 years later, we don't have an analog to Star Wars, which took aspects of Westerns, sci-fi serials, and fantasy to create something often imitated but never duplicated. Because of this, Aquatics are able to win by being the first person into a genre and riding a wave of success.

However, they often have problems explaining what they've done to people, which is why they are reliant on other ecosystems, like Deserts and Grasslands, to help bring in the masses to what they do or risk writing in obscurity without anyone knowing what they've done.

Each of these ecosystems is deeply committed to fostering a devoted audience and building a supportive community for them. However, *they do it in very different ways.*

Only Forests would find exceptional value in having a traditional Reddit forum, Facebook group, or paid membership community and fostering interactions between their fans. Their superpower is imbuing interconnectivity between books, and their career grows more successful with every member they add to the community, *so of course, that's what they love.*

I've watched healthy Forest communities in action, and they are a site to behold. However, that doesn't mean the other four ecosystems are broken or unable to build brand loyalty through their own community.

Tundras generally like to share cool things with their audience, so creating a mailing list to curate interesting stuff they find is perfect for them to interact with fans around common interests. Tim Ferris has used this exact strategy for years. Tundras also love marketing in short bursts, so conventions work particularly well for them. They might also benefit from a limited-time, cohort-based community focused around a launch.

Grasslands create a community around a topic, as everyone nerds out about the same thing with focused attention. They build community by leading people and being there to catch them when they fall. Content marketing is a perfect avenue for them to build community, using their own Substack, Medium, website, or another platform where they get the advantage of SEO and backlinks for years to come. Since they are always right about emerging topics, they can benefit the most from network effects, too, as the topic grows in importance and more people talk about it. They might also get a lot of value from a shared interest community built around their topic.

Aquatics are interested in creating lots of products to further the brand, so while they might have a community like Forests do, the way they interact with them will probably be by providing new experiences to their fans, not necessarily interacting with them on a personal level. Perhaps they could also build a product-centric community around their brand.

Meanwhile, if Deserts want to create a community at all (*and of all the types, Deserts are least likely to want to do that*), then they should probably join communities filled with readers where new trends are happening so they can interact directly with readers to collect data on what readers actually care about right now.

These are all communities and ways to develop deep, meaningful connections with people. ***They are all also equally valid depending on what works for you.***

When I think about building a healthy ecosystem, I often circle back to the 5 Love Languages.

I am a Tundra, and my love language is a combination of gift-giving and acts of service. So, when I think of my ideal ecosystem, it involves making things for people and demonstrating how much I care by sharing it with them in a grand gesture like a launch.

That is not the only framework I think about, though. I sit at the intersection of many different ones that inform each other. I'm a trailblazer in Becca Syme's Author Success Archetypes, which means I'm always out in front of new things. I'm also an Enneagram 8w7 non-conformist, which means I'm always challenging the status quo. My top five CliftonStrengths are Command, Strategic, Achiever, Communication, and Connectedness.

All of these combine to make me the kind of creator I am, and they work in tandem to inform my decisions.

I don't think I could live any peaceful existence if I didn't know all of those things about myself. It is the convergence of CliftonStrengths, Author Success Archetypes, Enneagrams, Love Languages, Author Ecosystems, and more that show me the overlapping Venn Diagram where I exist in ikigai.

We live in a world of personalization, and ***if that is true, then "the stack" is mercifully dead*** or at least evolving. I see a future where "the stack" means a collection of strategies you could use to be successful, but they need to be tailored to you. I hope "the stack" morphs into "the stacks" and, like the main bookshelves of a great library, represents a collection of potential paths forward, filled with endless possibilities to explore, instead of an oppressive pile of tactics that must be absorbed and regurgitated.

There are countless ways to be successful, and our goal should be to find the things that are uniquely relevant to us. I personally like the idea of a community flywheel, where

the community is the center point of our creative livelihood
, but the way it's described in this article would never work
for me. I need to adapt it to work for my business and
recognize that others might not resonate with it at all.

Moreover, *as a fan, the idea that there is only one right
way to be a good fan is insulting.* I do not want to engage
with random humans about the music I love. I want to buy
the album, listen to it by myself, geek out about it for a
minute with friends, and then sit with how it will
fundamentally change my existence as I listen a hundred
more times.

Most of the fans who financially support my work never
email me. They do not reply to emails. We do not engage
online. They don't answer polls. *That is not the
relationship we have, but it doesn't mean we don't care
about each other*. I show them cool things I've made, and
when those things resonate with them, they buy them if
they can or show some enthusiasm in some other way if
they can't. *We connect through the work, not because of it
or on top of it.*

That might not be your ideal process, and that's okay
because we live in a world where both are equally right and
wrong, depending on how they are deployed in your own
business.

Now, if you'll excuse me, I'm going to listen to Gag Order
a hundred more times before Friday.

ARE YOU FINDING ARBITRAGE OR BUILDING ARBITRAGE?

When I first started building my career in earnest, Gary Vee was using the term "attention arbitrage" to explain what people needed to be concerned with in the then-nascent creator economy. In short, **arbitrage results from a gap between demand and supply. If there is more demand than supply, the delta, or difference, between the two is arbitrage.**

I'll be honest: every time I heard that term for years, my teeth started gnashing together.

That said...he was right, and I hate that he was right. Since sucking it up and accepting he was right, though, I've identified two ways authors can use arbitrage in their own business. It's completely revolutionized how I think about my efforts.

Let's step back for a minute and talk about the way I define arbitrage. I define arbitrage as the *difference, or delta*, between *supply* and *demand*. When there is *more* demand than supply, then there is an arbitrage opportunity. Here are some examples of arbitrage as I would define it:

- A classic example in fintech is when you buy a stock at $.90 and flip around to sell it for $1.00. *That $.10 difference is arbitrage.*

- Similarly, often people buy products from a company like Costco or Trader Joe's for a 25-50% markup. *That markup is arbitrage.*
- When looking at authors, one classic example is K-lytics. Their entire business model is about showing authors emerging categories where the demand for a type of book exceeds their supply. *The difference between demand and supply is arbitrage.*

All three of those are classic arbitrage examples, but do you see the similarity between them? *They all deal with finding existing arbitrage.*

Each case above requires somebody to study data and find the gaps in the market where arbitrage exists. This is how a certain subset of authors, namely Deserts, operate naturally. They can identify an area where readers are almost frothing at the mouth for new books, write books for that market quickly to satisfy their needs, drop a book into that frenzied market, and use that excitement to profit.

Simply by existing, these books succeed. They don't need an audience. They don't need a popular author. They just need the audience to know about them, and they'll gobble it up.

That's great in the short term, but there is a huge problem with it, too. *Namely, if you find that arbitrage, somebody else will as well.* The minute you discover that opportunity, the clock is ticking before everyone else starts exploiting it, too, and that arbitrage dries up.

If you've ever been around authors who talk about how their books are not performing as well, their ads are not profitable anymore, or they need to hop genres because it's too crowded, in 99 out of 100 cases, they are feeling the squeeze of arbitrage drying up.

If an author finds a category that can support 1,000 books and there are only 100, that's a great arbitrage opportunity. However, what happens when more authors find that opportunity, and now there are 2,000 books in that category?

That's when you get more expensive ads, fewer readers clamoring for your book, longer waits for readers to find and read your book, and a whole slew of headaches that revolve around that arbitrage drying up. Once that happens, your only choice is to find another arbitrage opportunity and rinse and repeat forever, right?

That sounds exhausting, frankly. What if there was another way, though? This whole time, we've been talking about finding arbitrage, but *we can also create arbitrage for ourselves, and it provides a huge opportunity for writers.*

Neil Gaiman, Stephen King, Tim Ferris, Joyce Carol Oats, Nora Roberts, Elizabeth Gilbert…these are writers who never have to find arbitrage because they spend an inordinate amount of time building their names, creating their categories, and separating themselves from the pack.

Yes, you could define each one within a primary genre, but they are so much more than that as well. Tim Ferris wrote a book on outsourcing, cooking, and healthy living, as well as a coffee table book with advice from industry leaders. Sure, he's in the personal development category, but he's really in the Tim Ferris category.

Stephen King mostly writes horror, but he also wrote *The Green Mile* and *Fairy Tale*. Again, he's a category of one.

Building your own arbitrage is the best opportunity for sustainability because the supply of you is one, and if demand for your work grows over time, more people will spend more money on it.

While Deserts, and to a lesser extent Tundras, excelled at the last phase of the indie publishing journey, Grasslands, Forests, and Aquatics are primed to excel at the next phase of the self-publishing journey because they are all about separating themselves from the pack and creating their own arbitrage.

- *Grasslands* like Monica Leonelle, Terry Pratchett, Cassandra Clare, and George R.R. Martin write long, in-depth series and know their topic better than anyone.
- **Forests** like Stephen King, Brandon Sanderson, Neil Gaiman, and Colleen Hoover create a shared language and community for their readers to thrive through exploring common themes across their work.
- **Aquatics** like Stephanie Meyer, Stan Lee, and George Lucas delight readers with different formats and experiences that allow them to get lost in their rich universes.

As a Tundra, I've had to completely revamp my business in the past year to become more "flywheel" than "pump" because the way I've been doing things for years became exhausting and unsustainable.

In business, the *"pump"* and *"flywheel"* models represent two distinct approaches to growth and operations. *The pump model* requires continuous and often significant input or effort to produce results, similar to a manual pump needing constant operation to move water. It's characterized by direct actions like aggressive sales, and the outcomes cease as soon as the effort stops. For instance, a business relying heavily on continuous aggressive marketing or sales efforts to drive revenue follows the pump model.

In contrast, ***the flywheel model*** is akin to a heavy wheel that's tough to start but, once spinning, maintains momentum with minimal additional effort. This approach in business is about creating a self-sustaining system that becomes more efficient over time. Initially, it requires significant investment and effort, but as the system gains momentum, it requires less effort to maintain or grow. An example is a company investing in customer satisfaction, which eventually leads to word-of-mouth referrals, reducing the need for direct marketing efforts. The flywheel model thus symbolizes a cycle where initial hard work leads to easier, ongoing success.

There will always be opportunities to find arbitrage, but if you're sick of jumping from one niche to the next only to find your effort losing efficacy or becoming exhausted over time, then it's time to ask how you can dig deeper to build arbitrage for yourself.

I love how **Grasslands** think about this problem. Their whole strategy revolves around identifying an arbitrage opportunity 1-2 years out and then spending an inordinate amount of time becoming the expert on that topic, whether that means writing 100 blog posts or a 12-book series so that by the time the trend comes, they are already everywhere. ***That is how they win.***

Forests and **Aquatics**, in contrast, create something wholly new and spend their time fostering a community that grows and grows over time with people who resonate with what they've written until they become the dominant force in the little category they built from nothing into an unstoppable force.

Tundras combine evergreen trends to build an irresistible package that excites everyone, but they lack focus. Tundras want to launch and forget the minute the launch is over. If they want to take advantage of building their own arbitrage, they have to get better at threading all their launches into one narrative.

At Writer MBA, we've used Monica's prowess as a Grassland to identify two trends, Kickstarter and direct sales, and then my prowess as a Tundra to bring attention to our efforts. Tundras are often unfocused, launching and abandoning things, so having a common thread of Author Ecosystems, or even this publication, to keep my focus is very helpful. For my fiction work, I'm working on bringing all my work into one overarching concept called The Cosmic Weave that fosters community and topic dominance in the same way as Discworld did for Terry Pratchett.

I'm no longer willing to seek out arbitrage and wring it all out before the opportunity dries up, but I am interested in finding that arbitrage and using it to help build my own arbitrage, which I think is something **Deserts** are uniquely qualified to do.

In an ideal world, these two concepts work in tandem with each other. I recommend finding arbitrage opportunities that you can then leverage to bring people back to your own arbitrage. That's how we throw gasoline on the fire of our spark and grow faster.

There will always be arbitrage opportunities, and you don't have to be a well-known author to find them. So, if you're exhausted finding and exploiting them without ever feeling like you're getting ahead, maybe it's time to think about how you can focus on creating your own arbitrage instead of leveraging it from other people.

HOW TO GET OVER YOUR SALES PHOBIA

Even though it's critical to a business's success, most people hate the idea of selling their products. They fear people will hate them, find them annoying, and turn away from them. More importantly, they believe selling is "gross". This is especially true for Grasslands.

In this chapter, I'll hopefully show you how to overcome those mental blocks and see sales as not only an integral part of your success but also a fun way to build an engaged audience that loves your brand. Keep in mind as you read this that I'm a Tundra, so I have an unnaturally high affinity for standing up and seeing, "Did you know you could buy this?" *YMMV.*

DO I HAVE TO, THOUGH?

No. You **absolutely** do not have to learn this stuff. However, if you don't occasionally remind people they can buy things from you, then there is almost no chance you can build a critical mass of customers to make a go of it.

But maybe you don't really want to make a go of it, and that's cool. Maybe you finish this article and go, "Yup, I hate every word of that, and I'm never gonna do it."

Then, at least, you can stop beating yourself up about it. The first step to overcoming a problem is recognizing it exists, and fear of sales is a prominent problem for nearly everybody I've ever met.

Recognizing the problem and deciding not to do anything about it lifts a huge weight off your shoulders. ***It is a solution in and of itself.***

After all, I would contend that the biggest thing holding people back from achieving the level of success they covet isn't their ability to make something cool; it's the ability to find people to buy that cool thing.

Usually, they can make something cool just fine, but they're petrified about talking about it. They are petrified of people hating them, laughing at them, and shunning them. They've put their heart and soul into making something, and the idea that somebody won't like it paralyzes them.

Does that sound like you?

If so, then you're in good company because I've never met somebody who didn't have a little bit of that going on deep down in the bowels of their soul.

Even the best salespeople have it. Heck, I have it right now as I'm writing this article. I worry that you aren't going to like this article, that it won't be filled with enough value for you, and that you'll hate me for it.

The thought of it makes me bristle, but I soldier on anyway. *See, not long ago, I was right where you are.*

What makes it so much harder is that I know it will turn some people off. At least a dozen of you reading this right now will unsubscribe and write me off forever. I hope that it magnetizes more people than it turns off and it helps build a deeper bond with those who are already in my orbit.

It took a ton of inner work to get there, and it's still hard every time I hit publish, but it was so much harder before I started the type of work I'll talk about in this article.

I used to be horrible at sales. By 30, I failed three companies, all because of my hubris and inability to realize sales were an integral part of the game.

After my third company went under, I didn't have the money to try again, so I had to get a job.

At the time, the only job I was qualified to get was in sales because there are almost no qualifications required in sales except to sell things. They'll take anybody for a commission-only position, which was where I started.

At first, I was as bad at sales as I was at running a company. I bounced around to *a lot* of sales jobs in those first years until I eventually landed at one that showed me how to sell and why selling was important.

It changed everything for me. I went from a terrible salesperson to the best salesperson in the company almost overnight. I rose from salesperson to sales manager to running my own office in just a few months.

Then, I started my fourth company, Wannabe Press, and this time it didn't fail. In just a couple of years, we went from making a few thousand dollars to six figures a year, and it all started because I overcame my fear of sales and marketing. It's been almost ten years, and I still make a good living from it to this day.

A very smart person once told me that to be successful as a business, you must be good at two things: ***the thing you do and selling it.***

Business success is a function of both.

THE TWO QUESTIONS...

I have two questions for you. These questions can change your opinion of sales right now. I've seen more light bulbs go off after asking these questions than any single thing I've ever said in my life.

Are you ready? Here they are.

- **Do you think you are a good person?** I'm not talking about Mother Theresa or Gandhi-level good. I mean, do you generally feel you do the right thing, given the option? Do you help your friends and family? Do you watch for pedestrians when you drive? Do you generally do good in the world when given the choice?
- **Do you think the things you make can change lives?** Again, I'm not talking about earth-shattering changes here. I don't expect your products to light the world on fire and create a revolution that will bring about an era of global peace. However, do you believe that you can bring even a moment of joy into a person's life with the things you make? Do you think it can help somebody in a moment of darkness or add a moment of great joy?

If you answered yes to both of these questions, then you are under a moral imperative to tell as many people as possible about your products.

This is not a choice.

If you are a good person, and you believe your products can change lives, then you **must** tell as many people about them as possible so you can change as many lives as possible.

I know that might sound silly or hyperbolic, but it's **absolutely** the truth. I've seen it happen over and over again.

I'm not a famous author, but I have a loyal fanbase built from traveling the world with my books and spreading the message of my work.

I can't tell you how many times people have come up to my table and thanked me for writing a book because it helped them in an hour of need. I saw the joy in their faces when they talked to me about the book and the sincere gratitude in their eyes as they spoke.

What would have happened if that person hadn't seen my book? What would have happened if I wasn't there for them when they needed me?

I don't know for sure, but they wouldn't have had a positive experience with my book, that's for sure. Their life wouldn't have been changed for the better because of me.

That would have been horrible for both of us.

The truth of the matter is that what you do can change lives. The better you are at marketing and sales, the more lives you can change.

And you are obligated to change those lives if you can.

That's the trick about sales.

Sales isn't about selling. It's about finding people who need your work in the depths of their souls and showing it to them.

I call this "soul resonance selling", which is about finding people who resonate on the same frequency of weirdness as you, and it's much, much harder than pain point selling.

Imagine a book vibrating with the same frequency as your body, and simply touching it sends a jolt through you. That's what I'm talking about with soul resonance selling.

We have to bake that resonance deep into our work so that it calls out to the right people.

There are lots of people I don't like, but I listen to them because they are geniuses at solving certain problems.

I do not follow any fiction writers, memoirists, or creative non-fiction writers that I don't resonate with because why would I?

There are infinite books out there, and I don't need yours…except that I do need to feel seen, and soul resonance selling is about showing people they are seen in a deep and meaningful way.

This creates much more loyal fans of your work, but it's also a higher-order need.

YOU WILL GET REJECTED…A LOT.

That last bit should have gotten you motivated to talk to all the people, every single one of them in the entire universe.

For about three seconds.

Then, the butterflies in your stomach fluttered, and you dropped back down to Earth, right?

It hit you like a ton of bricks.

Because…if you have to talk to everybody, doesn't that mean you're going to get rejected by just about everybody? Doesn't it mean people are going to hate you?

Well, I have bad news and good news.

The bad news is, yes, you will have to talk to people, a lot of people. The good news is that almost none of them will hate you.

Most of them will nothing you.

They won't care about you at all.

Cheery, right? The creeping dread that most people don't care if you live or die isn't a comfortable one, is it?

The good news is there is even more good news.

The good news is that this happens to everybody. Almost nobody cares about even the most famous person you can imagine.

Think about Stephen King. There isn't a more famous author than Stephen King. He set the bar for success not only with his books but also with his movie adaptations for the past several decades.

He sells about 2 million books worldwide every time he releases something, like clockwork. ***That's a massive number, right?***

However, there are around 2 billion literate people in the world, which means 1.98 billion people don't buy his books.

Some might hate him, but most…just nothing him. Stephen King doesn't factor into their lives at all.

Or think about *The Walking Dead*…

…the smash hit television show racked up about 12 million viewers an episode at the height of its popularity…

However, there are over 200 million adults in America alone. This means 188 million people just…didn't care enough to watch.

I know that seems depressing, but the depressing part only exists if you look at who doesn't care about you. The trick is to focus on those that do.

Any network would kill to have a show with 12 million viewers.

Every author would love 2 million book sales every time they launched a book.

Those are phenomenal numbers, but they come with a ton of rejection.

If we focus on the rejection, we'll always be disappointed. However, if we focus on those who love our work and spend all our time finding more of them, then the rejection doesn't matter.

In fact, the more fans you get, the more rejection you face, and that's a good thing.

Because it's not about those people who don't care.

It's about the people who do, and every time you find somebody that doesn't care about your work, you are closer to finding one that does.

Rejection is a certainty in life, no matter what you do. The real trick is understanding that rejection gets you closer to acceptance with the right people, and that's what it's about in the end: connection.

WHO IS GOING TO BUY YOUR WORK?

Now that I've hopefully gotten you over your fears of rejection, it's time to ask the next logical question. Namely, who is even going to buy your stuff?

If you've been doing this for a while with very little success, then there's a good probability that you think that nobody is interested in the stuff that you sell.

If you haven't even started yet, then you're probably thinking that nobody will ever want to buy what you are going to make.

Does any of that sound familiar?

Well, I can tell you definitively that there *is* a market for what you are trying to sell.

How do I know?

Because there is a market for everything.

For proof, look at Temu or Alibaba. Most of the stuff on there doesn't make any logical sense, yet it must sell because they are advertising it. On top of that, I know a ton of people who make niche stuff and kill it.

- I know people who make nerdy oven mitts and make good money.
- I know people who sculpt weird, made-up animals and make good money.
- I know people who draw sad cartoon superheroes and make good money.

Except for maybe that last one, these are all obscure niches. There's no reason somebody should be able to make money on any of them.

And yet they do because there is a market for everything.

You just have to find it.

I'm going to hit you with a hard truth now.

You are not a special snowflake.

You are one of eight billion people on this planet.

Eight billion.

That's a ton of people, and it ensures that you are not alone in your weirdness. If you like something, there is a good bet that at least 10,000 other people like it, too. You just have to find them.

And that's the game.

Finding those 10,000 people as quickly as possible, and serving them enough awesome stuff that they will pay you to make cool stuff now and far into the distant future.

It's absolutely and fundamentally doable. When you look at it that way, it's almost inevitable, given that you put in the work.

What do you think? Can you put in that work? I think you can.

Now, we just have to figure out how to find them, which is what we'll talk about next.

WHY ARE YOU GIVING IT AWAY?

I've given away tens of thousands of books in my career to all sorts of people. I generally believe in giving my best stuff away and letting the universe figure out the rest. Somehow, it always works out in the end, but it only works because I know a secret.

The more knowledge I give away, the more trust I build with my audience, and trust is the key to sales. If I give away my best information, people are more likely to buy from me, not less.

It's because I'm not trying to sell people. I'm providing value to your life with no expectation of return. I know you have a pain point, and I'm filling it. That builds a lot of trust. I learned this from Grasslands, and this is a super Grassland trick. They are great at attracting new fans by providing value to their lives.

This realization turned everything around for me. The only sales I ever saw came from used car salesmen and stock brokers who would murder their mothers for a sale, and I hated that idea.

However, I do like to talk, and that became my biggest strength. I spoke to my customers forever, but instead of hard selling them, I would provide value and explain products. I would tell them why they should use our products and when they should go with a competitor.

Through that process, I made them comfortable with me because I helped them instead of forcing a product on them.

And, eventually, they would buy.

Well, at least some of them did—*enough for me to make a very good living.* I could never tell who would buy, but I figured out that if I talked to enough people, the math worked out in the end.

Most of them never bought, though. Most of you will never buy anything I sell either, and that's okay. Remember, it takes millions of people to lead to thousands of loyal fans.

The truth is that while I would love for you to buy what I make, that doesn't factor into how hard I work on what I give away. I'm trying just as hard to help you succeed whether you buy from me or not.

Will the people who buy my products and services get more value? Of course, they will, but only because those products are much longer than a free article and more focused on driving immediate results.

This is the mindset shift that you need to make in your own business if you think selling is gross. The truth is that selling can be gross, but helping people is never gross.

Unfortunately, most businesses are *sales first.* The first and last thing they care about are the numbers at the end of the day, no matter the cost.

99.9% of businesses work like this to their detriment.

True rock stars understand that to be great at sales, you must be *value first.* You must give information freely and openly.

You must do it consistently, honestly, and with the same effort whether somebody buys from you or not.

If you can do that, you'll no longer feel gross about sales, *and* you'll start seeing your network rapidly expand. You'll start seeing people *want* to buy from you instead of you needing to sell to them.

I call this the virtuous sales cycle. Every time I enter a new market, the path to success is pretty much the same. When I start a new venture, there is a little bit higher of a base for me to begin with, but not as much as you would think. This is the general breakdown of my path to success, which I call my virtuous sales cycle.

1. People are wary at first. They have been burned many times, and they aren't sure they can trust me. This is when I flood the market with free things because I want to show that my work is incredible. The more people who try my work, the more will get hooked on it.
2. People hesitantly try one of my products (books, comics, courses, etc.) for free, and most of them never read them. However, I keep giving them out to more and more people because a small percentage of those people will like what I have made.
3. It takes a long time before somebody dips their toe into my water to see what kind of things I create, usually about three to six months. Most people simply don't try it. This is a very slow time because

you can only push so hard. Mostly, you just have to wait, and it's horrible.

4. The people who tried and enjoyed my first product buy, or try for free, a second product of mine. They are still wary that they will not enjoy my work. After all, anybody can luck out once.

5. Those people try the second product more quickly than the first. This usually takes two to four weeks, or even less, as many people try the second product immediately. Some of those people don't like the second product, and their fears are confirmed. Others try it and like the second product and realize I'm not a one-trick pony.

6. At this point, I have developed fans for life. Once I can get somebody to try and love two different products, I have hooked them. They will go and try all my other products and fall in love over and over again. Those fans tell other people and rope them into buying from me.

7. Those new people who have been referred to me go through steps 2-6, and word starts to spread. My goal is to get as many people as possible through step 6 because that is when the referrals start to trickle in, and people start joining my ecosystem and moving through quickly. A referral from a friend is one of the most powerful marketing tools available.

8. There is an explosion of revenue every time I launch, as more and more people eagerly await what I have to sell, knowing I'm not going to disappoint them. This is the critical mass I am trying to build with every new venture, and I release products rapidly at the beginning so I can build this head of steam. Once I have built this steam, I can ease off the gas a little bit, knowing my fans will be waiting for me.

I have sold all kinds of things to people in all sorts of consumer service industries: phones, courses, comic books, novels, marketing services, and more. In every case, these steps have been the cycle for my success. It takes forever, which is where advertising helps bring in new people, but the results have been the same across every industry.

The key is making something great that delights people and then showing it to more and more people to get them excited about what I do. Once the referrals start rolling in, everything starts to snowball, and then it's time to put gas on the fire and find even more people.

This is my virtuous sales cycle of success.

Just because you give away information freely doesn't mean you don't do it strategically, though.

You must have a plan to move people from readers to buyers.

HOW DOES PROVIDING VALUE WORK?

Now, we've made the shift from a sales-first to a value-first mentality. Providing value builds trust between you and your audience, and trust leads people to buy from you.

While this value is critical to success, it's important not to provide it haphazardly.

It is essential to provide information for free, but we need to be strategic about the information we provide to make sure we are pointing people to where they can build a deeper connection with us…for a price.

This is called the value ladder.

The value ladder is a way to structure your business so that people can build a deeper relationship with you and obtain ever more impactful help with their problems for increasingly higher and higher price points.

For instance, people value individual help more than group coaching, group coaching more than a recorded course, a recorded course more than a book, and a book more than a blog post.

At each of those stages, people are getting more and more value, and in return, you can charge a bigger premium for each of these services you provide.

The first step on the value ladder is free content delivered consistently and without the expectation of somebody buying from you.

This content can be delivered in the form of a weekly blog, a podcast, or a video on any one of a hundred platforms.

In general, you will likely choose one of the following as your main medium for delivering content.

- **Blog Posts/Articles:** If you like writing, you might choose written articles or blog posts. These are the original currency of the internet. Personally, this is what I use for my main content delivery. While we have a podcast and produce video content, it is sporadic compared to our written content.
- **Videos:** The internet seems to have moved to a video-first medium, and with it, left me behind because I do not do well on video. This includes vlogs, educational videos, interviews, or even animated content. Video engages audiences and often receives high interaction rates.

- **Podcasts/Audio Content:** My favorite medium (*though one I simply don't have much time or energy for*) is podcasting, specifically the interview podcast. I recorded 200 episodes of my previous podcast, and it built so many ***amazing connections.***

This format allows authors to explore topics through discussions, interviews, or storytelling. It's a great way to reach audiences who prefer audio content.

That's not to say you can't create in all three formats, but one will be the one you build from the most and use as the main driver of your growth. The biggest thing you can get from a main format is consistency. I know I will write articles every week because I have done it since 2008. The other formats have come and gone, but writing has stayed consistent, which means I can **consistently deliver it.**

This can be used for non-fiction authors, but a fiction author can create a web serial, an audio drama, a web series, or any number of free offers to bring people into your universe.

This content should help your audience but also relate to products that you offer in your business.

The idea of free content is that people say, "Wow! If this is what they're giving away for free, what must their paid content be like?"

This will lead to somebody opting into your email list. Usually, you will need to offer something like a free book or another piece of exclusive content to get people onto your mailing list, but if you have a banger publication, often they will opt in because they don't want to miss anything you post.

Once they are on your list, the next step on your value ladder is called the "tripwire offer". This is an offer that doesn't cost very much but turns somebody from a consumer of your work into a buyer of your work.

The tripwire offer is possibly the most important of all your offers. Once somebody is a buyer of your products, it's 10x easier to sell them your next product. Getting somebody to buy the first time is the hardest part, which is why we offer heavy discounts and trials to get people in the door.

The next rung on your value ladder should be more expensive and give even more value, and it should continue the same way with every subsequent rung.

That is the secret to the value ladder and free content in general.

It's not about just making the content free. It's about delivering value to somebody who has a need, helping them, and offering a way to get even more help by developing a deeper relationship with you.

This isn't about telling people to buy your products, though. It's about helping them and giving them the epiphany they need your work in their life. *People buy when they have an epiphany.*

THE EPIPHANY...

You can't force a customer to buy your products. You can inform them, enlighten them, and instruct them about what they need, but at some point, the choice is up to the customer.

They must be the ones to take their money and exchange it for your products. They only do that once they have the epiphany that they need your offer.

What is an epiphany?

You know when you're watching a cartoon, and somebody is trying to find a solution to a problem? They think hard for a few moments, then a light bulb goes off over their head, and they suddenly know exactly what to do.

That is them having an epiphany.

Our goal is to create an environment where the right customers have an epiphany that they need our products as soon as possible.

One way we do this is by using psychological buying triggers. These buying triggers are subtle ways to get customers to have the epiphany that you are right for them.

There are dozens of buying triggers, but I've boiled them down to the six most important that you need to know to get started.

- **Reciprocity**—When you give something to somebody, they are more likely to want to give something back to you. This is one of the main drivers behind providing free, valuable content to people.
- **Authority**—When somebody is an expert in their space, you are more likely to buy from them. It's very hard to become an expert, and if you can show expertise in a subject, people will trust you more and will spend money with you.
- **Consistency**—The more often you show up, and the longer you show up, the more people will trust

you. The simple act of being around somebody improves your opinion of that person.

- **Commitment**—Whenever somebody engages with your brand, be it through opening emails, liking photos, or even finding you at live events, they are recommitting their interest in your brand and thus reaffirming their trust in you.
- **Social Proof**—When somebody's friends buy something, they are more likely to buy it, too. This is where having quality reviews and testimonials on your site helps drive sales. People trust what other people are buying.
- **Scarcity**—When a deal goes away, people are more likely to buy it before it vanishes. This is why you see so many limited-time offers and flash sales because the scarcity convinces people to get off the fence and buy immediately. It doesn't help build trust as much as make people act on the trust that's already been built up over time.

By adding these buying triggers into your existing practices, you can enforce people's commitment to your brand, their trust in you, and their desire to enter deeper into your ecosystem by purchasing products from you.

Each of these buying triggers is incredibly powerful by itself, but when you stack them together, you can see exponential results.

For example, a person who gets a daily email from you after opting into your mailing list to receive a free eBook will receive **consistency** from your emails, build **commitment** by reading your emails, see you as an **authority** as you deliver value, and want to **reciprocate** the generosity of your free eBook, thus engaging four powerful buying triggers at once.

The more of these buying triggers you can engage, and the longer you can engage them, the more rabid your fan base will become.

GETTING PEOPLE TO TRUST YOU...

Now that we've learned all about getting the right people to trust you, let's talk about building a repeatable system to turn somebody who doesn't know you into a raving fan. Rest assured, there is a system.

It's called a sales funnel.

The sales funnel works like an upside-down triangle, wherein a lot of people go into the top, and eventually, most of them funnel out, leaving only the fraction left willing to buy your work.

Just like buying triggers, there are dozens of ways to design a sales funnel, and they can mean many things to many people.

I have distilled the sales funnel down to its most basic five steps, which you need to know right now to be successful.

- **KNOW**—This is the process of finding people and bringing them into your ecosystem. Before this step, customers have no idea who you are. Afterward, they are part of your community.
- **LIKE**—After people know who you are, you must show them you are a likable human by talking about yourself, helping them with their problems, and generally creating empathy between you and them.
- **TRUST**—After somebody likes you, the next step is convincing them you make amazing products. This involves showing them what you make,

pointing them to amazing reviews, letting them try out your products, etc. The goal is to make them trust that not only are you a good person but that you make a great product.

- **BUY**—Once people trust you, they should be ready to buy from you when the need arises for your product in their lives. Hopefully, you've brought people into your ecosystem who already need your product immediately, but often, people will sit for months without buying until a pressing need arises. This is where the scarcity buying trigger comes into play.
- **BUY AGAIN**—Once somebody buys from you, it's important to deliver an amazing product, even overdelivering, so people are willing to purchase from you again and again. It's 10 times easier to keep an existing customer than to find a new customer, and these customers will be the base of your business in the future.

I like to think of the funnel like this:

We all have that uncle we **know** but don't **like**…

…that cousin we **like** but don't **trust**…

…and that friend who we **trust** but won't give money to because they have different tastes.

However, we also have that best friend to whom we'll gladly give money all the time because they always come back with the coolest stuff, whether it's food or concert tickets. You love everything they suggest.

Your job is to be best friends with as many people as possible so they will gladly give you their money.

Tundras and Deserts are amazing at this but suck at creating a flywheel, which is how to nurture leads and customers so they become repeat customers. Meanwhile, Grasslands, Forests, and Aquatics are all about the flywheel and suck at actually standing up and saying, "Did you know you can buy this?", which is why they desperately need a funnel.

WHAT IF THEY'RE STILL NOT BUYING?

There is a chance that you'll get your funnel set up, and people still won't buy from you. Then you'll come back to these paragraphs and...be so angry with me for wasting your time.

Luckily, there are only a couple of main reasons this could be happening, and simple corrections can easily rectify the flaws in your design.

The most pressing reason you still aren't making sales is that you aren't asking for them. Most business owners aren't giving their customers a reason to buy from them nearly enough.

If you're a Grassland, Forest, or Aquatic, it probably feels like I just punched you in the mouth, but it's true. ***Customers are not mind readers.*** While they are interested in your products, there are a thousand things that draw their attention every day.

If you tell them that there is a new product or some deal, chances are good that they will buy that product...given that you have made something that interests them.

The second possible reason that you aren't making sales is that you are collecting potential customers, but you aren't reaching out to them often enough to make a connection.

Customers need to hear from you every week to keep your brand in the forefront of their minds. If you reach out monthly or even less frequently, people will forget about you.

I'm specifically talking about reaching out with value-based content here. You don't need something to sell every week, and it's probably better if you don't, but to stay top of mind with people, you should be reaching their inboxes regularly.

If you are sitting on emails you've collected without reaching out, it means you aren't nurturing your audience. Even if those people were interested at one point, they quickly moved on to another product when you ignored them.

The next thing you might be doing is bombarding people with pleas to buy your products too often. This is the inverse of the problem above. If you are constantly telling people to buy, then your pleas become white noise. Remember, the people in your audience are more than just $20 bills.

You wouldn't constantly harass your best friend to buy something from you, and you shouldn't beg your audience to buy from you all the time, either. It's annoying.

You must walk a delicate balance between launching too much and giving people enough chances to buy from you.

Because people do want to buy. They are consumers living in a consumerist culture. However, they don't want to be pestered. If you're reaching out with an offer, every email should come from a different angle and add to their knowledge of what you're selling.

For instance, if you're selling a book, then your first email should talk about the book, then the main characters, then the world, then the villain, and keep building out the lore throughout the launch sequence so customers fall deeper in love with your work *until they have an epiphany.*

Everything you do as a business is about nurturing a customer until they have an epiphany and decide to buy.

Another possible option is that you aren't feeding enough people into the top of your funnel to create enough buyers to sustain yourself.

Only a small fraction of people who make it into the top of your funnel will turn into buyers at the bottom, so if you aren't filling the top with a lot of people, it's very hard to churn out enough buyers at the bottom to sustain yourself financially. If you're converting 1-2% of your leads into customers, you're doing decently. Anything under 1% is a problem. Anything above 5% means you probably aren't expanding your audience wide enough.

There is one more option, and that is you are reaching out enough and have enough people in your funnel, but you've built a list of people who aren't interested in what you sell.

This happens if you run unspecific lead gen offers targeted at everybody instead of honing them specifically for your ideal customer. The things you offer for free should be congruent with the things you are selling. If they are not, your email list will not convert into buyers, and you'll have to build it from scratch, as I did with my Twitter account and my first Instagram account.

It is important to fill your funnel with a lot of people, but it's equally important to make sure you have the right kind of people in your ecosystem who are interested in buying what you sell.

These are the most common reasons you still aren't making money on your funnel. If you can fix and tweak them, you'll be well on your way to success.

HOW TO USE TECHNOLOGY AND PRODUCTIVITY HACKS TO RECLAIM YOUR TIME FOR THINGS THAT MATTER

I think about whisks a lot. ***Yes, those kinds of whisks***. The ones you use to whip eggs and do basic cooking tasks. Did you know that before the 19th century, whisks were basically just a bunch of sticks and thatch bundled together ?

Think about how inefficient it would be to use a bunch of sticks to stir ingredients together. It took forever, and it severely limited the types of recipes that could realistically be executed on any given day.

Then, in the 19th century, this magical invention came onto the scene that promised to make cooking significantly easier and lower the bar for kitchen chefs everywhere. ***Except…that's not what happened.***

Instead of making existing recipes more efficient and making cooking take less time, what actually happened was the bar was raised for what was expected for the average cook to create on any given day. Out with cake, in with souffle.

Since cooking dinner was historically a burden overwhelmingly carried by women, so was this new expectation disproportionally carried by them. *That doesn't really have specific relevance here, except it pisses me off every time I hear it.* This burden extended beyond the making of the recipe, too, as cooks had to learn how to create these new recipes and test them to make sure they didn't burn the whole house down in the process. When technology advanced from whisks to mechanical egg beaters onward to electric ones, those demands only increased.

This was not an isolated incident, either. Refrigeration had a similar cost burden, as instead of going to the store every day to find what was fresh and in stock, cooks now had nearly infinite choices at their disposal from around the world, which raised the expectations for the types of cuisine to cook. Even the humble stove made it so that you didn't have to stand over a flame all day, but still, cooks spent the same amount of time cooking as they had a century before.

I am not a Luddite, but I do think they were onto something. Used as a slur in today's day and age, the Luddites arose as a reaction to technology threatening their livelihoods.

About once a week, I get the overwhelming urge to smash some piece of technology, so I have respect for an organization that saw through the bull promising that technology was guaranteed to improve their lives. Yes, there are some great ways that technology has undoubtedly changed the world for the better. Two hundred years ago, 80% of the world lived in extreme poverty. Today it's 8%. During that same time, life expectancy has more than doubled.

People suffer less now, even if it doesn't feel that way. Still, if everything is better, why do we have less time than our forefathers? Humanity historically worked 15 hours a week for most of our existence, yet with every new advancement, we become more "productive" without gaining any time. Now, we're working 60-80 hours a week to keep our heads about water. Part of that is capitalism, which is silly, but another big part of this is technology promising to save us time when, in practice, it just raises expectations and alienates us from everyone around us.

Yet, technology marches on. AI is the new(ish) technology on the block, promising to save us time and money by automating much of our lives. However, instead of allowing people to work 15 hours a week, employers are expecting exponentially more output from the same amount of time.

This is also true with creative entrepreneurs. They are constantly pulled in a hundred different directions, trying to stay afloat, yet it is never enough. This is in no small part due to capitalism feeding off creatives like a vampire.

Creators literally create the growth mechanism for platforms to turn a profit and then are shut out of the process after years of work. They are told to toil away for endless hours to create content that can be monetized "eventually". Meanwhile, they are actually too fried to make the things they love. Then, the owners drive the platform into the ground to extract maximum value for shareholders at the expense of their users, destroying all the goodwill creators have built up over the years.

That's why I literally don't care what the platform is. I won't even try it unless I control the data. Maybe I will go and run ads on them to pull my fans out, but I won't do any work to add value to them if they are going to charge me to access the very value we help them build.

It's a problem that goes back all the way to the humble whisk, a harbinger of doom for all technological innovations to come. It doesn't have to be that way, though. Many strategies can help us reclaim our time, even as new technology like AI looms large over everything we do these days.

If you are too busy to do the things you like and can never get ahead, you are over-leveraged and in time debt. To get out of that debt, you need to find leverage points in your business to exploit.

If you are overleveraged, then you are most likely focused on too many low-margin activities, the kind of thing you can train somebody else to do and have nothing to do with your zone of genius. These are admin, customer service, data entry, and other tasks that are required to keep your business functioning but that you don't personally have to do for your business to keep running.

These are called $5 tasks because you can hire them out for about $5-$15 (This is an old metric but still works to describe entry-level tasks). These are also the tasks that AI is best poised to handle right now. Whether it is setting meetings, doing tedious research, spell-checking your work , helping with book marketing, or any number of low-level but necessary tasks, there is AI to help you do them better so you can reclaim large swaths of time.

You are probably (mostly) focused on $50 tasks. This is you being a technician in your business. This is the writing, drawing, editing, etc, that turns your ideas into books and articles. You may think you cannot hire these tasks out, but you can probably hire parts of them. AI is much worse at doing this type of work, though corporations seem to believe this is the future because they are stonewalling writers for demanding their work isn't used to train their replacements.

It's true that nobody can write quite like you, but you can hire editors, proofreaders, cover artists, etc.. As a comic book artist, you may need to do line work for a project but can hire out flatting, lettering, coloring, and inking. Or you can do your linework digitally and not pencil at all to create more time.

I know this sounds expensive, but it allows you more time to do better work that will pay you more, and it allows you to turn around projects faster, which generates more revenue for your business.

If you don't want to hire out, then you could increase productivity on each of those tasks. For instance, I increased my daily output from 1,000 words to 5,000 words without decreased quality, so I now finish a book in a fraction of the time, saving more time. You can also use AI to help you flesh out certain aspects of your writing and add things you might miss. This might turn your stomach initially, but programmers have used AI to help them write code for years.

Another thing you can do is get existing clients to pay more. I know people generally hate raising their rates, but if you can double your rates and still retain 60% of your business, you are still ahead of the game. Plus, you have reclaimed half your time without decreasing your revenue.

If you aren't comfortable doubling your rates off the bat, try increasing your rates by 10%-25% every quarter until you start seeing people balk at your new pricing. If you have a good relationship and communicate with your clients, they will generally be willing to pay more for your services to retain you.

Or you can decrease the churn in your business so more people stay year after year. Most creative businesses are not concerned with churn enough. If you know that 20% of your customers leave every year, and you can find a way to cut that to 10%, you have just removed the need to spend marketing dollars and time onboarding new clients by 50%.

Still, *$50 tasks should not be the end goal of your creative business*. When you are stuck at the $50 activities (*or, even worse, $5 activities*) in your business, the things you are definitely not focused on are the tasks that will grow your business, and those are the $500+ tasks.

These are the strategic partnerships you form and the products you launch with better results every single time. *These $500+ tasks are ways you can double your income while halving your workload.* They are the processes you put in place to offload your work so that you can take on more clients. These $500+ tasks are how you create leverage by productizing services, creating new products, or outsourcing.

I am not a particularly hard worker. *I am just very good at finding leverage points and knocking over dominos.* People are often surprised when I tell them how little I actually work because I generally seem so busy. But that is because I am excellent at leveraging myself and creating space to say yes to great opportunities and turning down bad ones.

It is possible to make the same money in 4 hours a day as you can in 16, and it is possible to create massive revenue in a very short amount of time. You just have to leverage yourself properly. It breaks my heart to see how so many people I know work without getting any gain.

In April 2018, I spent two amazing weeks on a book tour in Spain. During that time, I did many incredible things, but one I will never forget is that I got the opportunity to eat at a couple of Michelin-star restaurants while we were in San Sebastian.

One of them was called A Fuego Negro. Aside from the puppets with penises that adorned the wall, I remember it as the best meal I've ever had in my life. Fifteen courses of amazing food played like a record across my palette. I couldn't believe how good that meal was, honest and true. It was perfection. Honestly, I never knew a meal could be so good.

On the menu, they had the year each course was added to the menu. The restaurant was over 10 years old, and there were pieces on the menu that spanned all of them, like the greatest hits of their past.

I'm sure the restaurant was amazing when it opened, but to deliver a world-class meal, it took ten years of refinement. It meant cutting really good menu items and replacing them with something great.

I run my business in a rather similar way. Every year, I take December off to examine everything I have tried in the past twelve months…and scrap everything that wasn't pulling its weight, even if it worked in the past.

Through that process, I've jettisoned some really good strategies for growing my business to make way for great ones. I let go of things that worked well enough to keep me going to *find ones that were world-class.*

Since I only have so much brainpower and bandwidth, I was left asking if it would be okay to stay at the level I was at for the next 10 years. Since it wasn't, I was forced to abandon things that were working decently.

Over the last few years, I've been able to construct a suite of world-class tools. There is still refinement to do to make it work perfectly, but there's no doubt it's working better than it ever has before.

An ecosystem is fragile. Introduce the wrong animals or vegetation, and it could send a perfectly balanced system into chaos. The same is true with any industry or even in your own practice.

Too often, people take on every responsibility thrown at them, whether it's ideas for books, potential partnerships, conventions, or marketing efforts, without any thought as to how it will affect their ecosystem.

Part of this is naivete.

At the beginning of your career, you literally don't know how your ecosystem works. You also don't have the opportunity to turn down much work without setting yourself back.

So, you take on more and more.

Then, you establish yourself but never take the time to figure out how your ecosystem works. So you continue throwing junk and trash into your ecosystem until it is on the verge of destruction, leading to burnout or worse.

To find equilibrium with yourself, you must find a balance that is right for you, jettisoning things that don't serve you, doubling down on things that light you up, and having enough space to recover.

The same is true when trying to place yourself in an industry. Whether it's comics, book publishing, magazines, or the world of food trucks, you need to find a way to become a beneficial part of the ecosystem...

...because if you aren't, then the ecosystem will treat you as a cancerous growth to protect itself against, and it will be very hard to make headway.

As you go about building your career, tasks will arise that threaten to eat into your precious creating time—Meetings, interview requests, guest articles, upcoming launches, and more start to creep into your day, demanding your attention.

That is why you must be precious of the time you have to create and hold it sacred above everything else. If you don't make it a habit from the beginning, it becomes nearly impossible to do it when other commitments start to intrude on it.

I'm a huge fan of time blocking and recommend it to any creative looking to protect their time. I generally use a time-blocking strategy that involves green time, yellow time, and red time.

With time blocking, you literally block out your schedule every day. Green time actions are ones that directly make you money. Maybe that's working on a Kickstarter campaign, running ads, or writing your book. Nothing impedes green time activities. However, green time activities can spill over onto yellow and red time.

Yellow time is admin time or something that indirectly leads to making money. Red time activities have nothing to do with your business.

The bottom line is that not all time is created equal. Some time is used on useless tasks. Some time is used for rest. Some time is used for making money. Some time is used for chores. We make the mistake of equating time equally, but *it is decidedly not equal*.

One surefire way to burnout is doing too many low-value tasks and not enough high-value ones. I know, for instance, that writing and resting are high-value tasks for me. Writing makes me money. Reading helps me recover.

Everything else in my business is secondary to those two tasks. Notice that only one of them directly makes me money (writing books), but the other is essential for my writing process to exist in harmony.

One of the best ways to reclaim your time is to stop splitting it between many different projects. Nearly every writer I know wants to write everything, everywhere, all at once, but if you want to leverage your time, it behooves you to push on one pressure point until you burst through the other side.

The simple fact is that multi-tasking takes *more* energy than single-tasking and has compounding negative effects. Suddenly, because your attention is elsewhere, simple tasks take longer than they should, throwing off your daily scheduleand stressing you out because you fall behind.

When you fully focus on a single task, however, you feel less stressand can even enjoy your work. Multi-tasking takes more energy than doing one task because of context switching. Just like how it takes more gas to start a car than to keep it running, starting up new activities costs more energy than doing one single task.

This focus extends beyond your daily schedule, too. The more focus you can put into any one area of your business, the more progress you will make on it.

I'm not talking about just focusing on a format like books or growing your Substack, either. I'm saying you should focus on one genre and hyperfocus yourself on breaking through one little gap in the market.

You might write 100 articles on one topic or write a 10-book signature series, but you are putting an overwhelming focus on a singular subject until people take notice and recognize you as remarkable.

When we focus our attention on one problem, everything we do amplifies each other. Otherwise, you will likely disburse your effort to such a degree that it will be hard to get anywhere.

Yes, you can step out of that box, but it's basically like starting your career all over again when you do. Some people will follow you between genres and formats, but most won't, and unless you have a huge audience, it's really hard to have enough of them willing to read your other stuff to make it profitable.

When you write in one genre, everything you release helps market and amplify everything else. When you work in a lot of different genres, your marketing doesn't really build on each other, or it takes a lot longer to work because you are not taking advantage of compound marketing. Compound marketing is the idea that you start with low-risk activities and build them on top of each other over time, with each action compounding on the last.

This is a Grassland-focused marketing strategy, but it can work for every ecosystem. Deserts are nimble enough to hop between genres, but they would benefit from diving deep into one main genre and getting to know the readers so well that they can predict trends better and spot them earlier.

Tundras can use this strategy to drive audience engagement with each book in a series as they build excitement for a launch.

Forests can use compound marketing to find faster success with one series that they can use to connect readers to all their work.

Aquatics can use it to quickly grow the audience for their overall brand when breaking into new markets.

I recommend always being underleveraged with your time and energy while trying to make every action you take increase the leverage you have in your business. This is how we protect our energy and make sure we always have a reserve of energy that builds over time.

Have you ever heard of a "profit first" mentality?

It's the idea that you take 10% off the top of your revenue for profit, and then you work with the remaining 90%.

I think in authorship, we need an "energy first" mentality, which means before we take on any project, we figure out how to retain 10% of our energy as "profit", so we always have some in the bank, investing and growing for us.

I am as bad at this as anyone (on both the profit and energy fronts). I was just about to go on sabbatical this year, and instead, I started a company with Monica that took all my energy.

I thought this year was going to be about restoration, and it instead became about transformation.

I'm not complaining about this year.

I have done so much, both physically and mentally, that changed me for the better and brought me to levels I've been struggling to get to for years. I've never eclipsed $150,000 in revenue until 2022, and in 2023, we more than doubled that number.

That's in no small part thanks to your support.

However, next year, I want to recover and make sure I always keep 10% of my energy just for me, so I'm building up a bank that will never run dry again.

Thinking, "Will I be able to run an energy profit after taking it on?" seems like a good enough place to start, as any.

You can use this "energy first" mindset to analyze what you can do with ease and then tack your expectations to that.

One of the things that changed my outlook on running a creative business was transitioning from overleveraging myself to being underleveraged, leaving huge gaps in my day for just thinking. This time allows me to find my most highly leveraged activities and double down on them.

Now, when something comes along that's a "heck yes", I have time for it. Meanwhile, *my income hasn't dipped because I have successively found more leveraged activities that continuously allow me to do more in less time.*

Humans are very good at filling out time with things that "might be fun" or "could be interesting", and then when something comes along that's a "heck yes!" they don't have the available time to do it.

Why do we do that? It turns out that humans are also very bad at projecting how they will feel in the future, which leads us to be mean to our future selves.

Chronic illnesses taught me that you have to reserve your spoons for the things that you really want to dobecause there are only so many hours in a day, and if you spend your spoons on things that are just okay, you won't have anything left for the stuff that you really want to do.

We are told to do all the things, but doing almost none of the things is way better until they resonate deeply. This mentality has gotten me further than doing all the things ever has.

So, should you even care about AI? Yes and no. AI probably will allow us to be more efficient, but will it provide us with more time in our day for enjoyment? *Only if we intentionally decide to use it that way.* Even now, I hear people talking about using AI to write books 10x faster or deliver bigger, longer, more in-depth articles than ever before.

And yes, that's all possible, but *it sounds exhausting and untenable*. I really appreciate Steph Pajonas's work on this subject because she has limited time and energy as well. So, she uses AI to create a life she loves and make the work that matters to her without overextending herself. I take a more measured approach to AI, but I tend to remain optimistic about its potential.

That said, the biggest problem with AI is that it is run, funded, and maintained by capitalists, and the hypercapitalism quagmire we find ourselves mired in exists solely to squeeze maximum profitability out of a system. Not to mention that AI doesn't need to be good to be weaponized against creatives, so I remain hesitant.

Like all technology, AI will only help insomuch as it allows you to gain more control over your life. ***That is true with anything, though, even the humble whisk.***

SPINNING A GREAT IDEA INTO BOOK MARKETING GOLD

I find it hard to develop a shared language about how difficult it is to create and launch creative projects.

I've called it "soul-selling", which is NOT selling your soul, but that's what everyone equated it to, so I stopped saying it.

I've called it heart selling, emotional selling, and a whole lot of other things that fell on stone-faced creative people over the years, mostly because when you combine the word sell with creative work, half the people (***and nearly all the people who need to hear it***) prickle up.

Recently, I saw *Spinning Gold*, though, and in it, I saw the parable about writing I had been looking for my entire life (minus the sex, the drugs, and the music). I often find my marketing inspiration in music, and that movie is a masterclass on what it means to introduce creative work to the world.

Maybe it's because I also grew up on the East Coast and fled to Los Angeles, or because I spent a decade failing and failing until people finally saw the value of what I had to say and everything started falling in place, but the story of Casablanca Records resonated deeply with me.

Music, at the end of the day, has the same intrinsic problems as fiction. At its core, nothing about music is necessary. It won't help you file your taxes. It won't help you lose 40 lbs in 40 days. It won't invest your 401k for you.

There is nothing intrinsic to music that people need, and the same is true with fiction books. In fact, people devalue both in almost the same way.

No, music is not necessary, but it is essential to life in the same way books are essential. To go into the arts and make it a career, you must be a little bit crazy because you're essentially selling air.

We talked about the "Blue Ocean Strategy" before. The book business is the opposite of that. The publishing industry is the reddest ocean you'll ever find, infested with thousands of hungry sharks. Over a million books are launched every year.

Every single author is trying to get people to read their books at the same time, including the estates of long-dead authors and publishers relaunching public domain books, and they're willing to drop their prices to nothing to capture them.

The last thing you want to do as a new business is to compete on price. As a small business, you don't have the scale to drop your prices or the name recognition to have intrinsic virality, but that's the common wisdom in the publishing business. Drop your prices to zero and make the money up in volume.

This is the general wisdom of selling books.

- **STEP 1:** Make a book.

- **STEP 2:** Drop the price as close to $0 as possible.
- **STEP 3:** ???
- **STEP 4:** Profit.

In the self-publishing world, this process works best when you have a long series because you can drop the first book in the series to zero and "make it up on read-through".

The more volumes you have in the series "behind" the free book, the more money you can make on the subsequent books and, thus, the more you can spend on advertising. The golden rule of book marketing is that the person who can spend the most on marketing wins.

The only people who get ahead in that world are the ones who have the most money to spend on marketing. Casablanca Records was $6 million in debt (in 1975 money. *That's over $33 million today*) before they turned it around, and they only got that much cash because Neil Bogart was a successful recording artist and record executive with connections as deep as anyone in music before he started his label.

How many people on Earth could have made that work back then? 10, maybe? Probably fewer…

Here's the thing, though. *Even with all its advantages, Casablanca Records barely succeeded.* They were down to their last dime when they turned it around and became the most successful indie label of all time. Yes, they eventually sold half their company for $50 million, but they almost flamed out.

They had a low, low, low probability of success and more money than God to dump into marketing until their record caught on, which is why having a runway is so important.

The longer you can keep doing your work and sharing it around, the longer you have to find a hit to keep yourself in business. You don't have to sell your soul to the mob to succeed, either, but you need to find ways to at least break even while you search for your hits.

So, as a new author, you now somehow need to write a long series (at least five books if you want the best chance of breaking even on ads) and enough money in the bank to find your hit…all at a time when 80% of people are living paycheck to paycheck.

If this is starting to feel like the deck is stacked against you…it is.

When I talk to publishers, we often talk about how publishing is a game of attrition. You are working to break even on projects and keep the lights on for years until you get a massive hit.

I have a friend who had to wait nearly 20 years for the hit that allowed them to 10x their business in a few years. I have another friend who had only had 2 hits since they opened, but those books sold millions upon millions of books.

In previous generations, the rule was that when you release 10 books, one of them paid for the other nine.

I don't think that's possible anymore. It really wasn't ever possible, but survivorship bias is a killer. For every successful publisher that survived for 10+ years, I talk to a dozen that flamed out and a hundred others that never even got started.

At Wannabe Press, we have to break even on every book and have from the beginning. When we got started, *Katrina*

Hates the Dead kept me in business for years, but my other books still sold enough to become profitable. They each paid for themselves, and Katrina paid for our expansion. Some months, those other books saved me.

On top of that, they only saved me because I had written off that money years before, so it was all found money to me.

The sole reason we even got to the point where *Katrina Hates the Dead* could keep us afloat was because I produced both that book and *Ichabod Jones: Monster Hunter* volume 1, along with 4 other books, years before I launched the company.

I made them while I was still working a full-time job, and after I received an insurance settlement that allowed me to pay off all our debt. I had already absorbed their cost years before I ever launched my company.

Without all of that, Wannabe Press never would have gotten off the ground. Even with those things working in my favor, by the time we started making money from these books, I had spent all our money, and then some, investing in products no publisher wanted, just like Neil Bogart and Casablanca Records.

By the time I officially launched Wannabe Press in 2015, our savings were completely depleted. It took living hand-to-mouth until 2017, before we found a hit and started getting ahead. It was only because my wife had a good job and I somehow lucked into ownership of a Verizon dealership when I left my job that the company survived until fans took notice.

This is a hard thing, and doing hard things is hard. It's hard to do creative work even if you are bound to fail at it, let alone succeed. I come from a middle-class family. I graduated from school with no debt. I married a woman who graduated from school with no debt. Our families were supportive of us, both emotionally and financially, when we struggled. We didn't have any children, and we didn't have any major life events that hampered us or illnesses that prevented us from moving forward…

…and still, with all of that…I almost failed.

It wasn't until the middle of 2022 that I thought maybe, just maybe, I wouldn't have to find a job in the next six months to survive. ***As recently as last March 2023, I was substitute teaching to supplement my income.*** Even now, my success is derived from multiple sources of income beyond fiction.

It took almost ten years of doing this work at a very, very high level, and a decade before then spent learning the trade, that I found any comfort in my position, and even now, I am cognizant of the fact it could all go away tomorrow.

By the time I turned it around, our company had burned through $100,000. We weren't $100,000 in debt, but only because of everything I mentioned above and about a thousand lucky breaks. That's not quite $33 million in debt, but it's a lot of money.

It took living on a razor's edge, robbing Peter to pay Paul, to get *Katrina Hates the Dead* off the ground. It took seven years for *Ichabod Jones: Monster Hunter* to find an audience. It took gambling everything on numerous 50/50 shots and winning a dozen times in a row to get here.

When *Monsters and Other Scary Shit* became an actual hit in 2017, we had literally gambled everything on it and our upcoming *Pixie Dust* release. If they didn't work…I don't know what we would have done. Their success allowed us to keep going until *Cthulhu is Hard to Spell* became our biggest hit ever and proved we had staying power.

It turns out you absolutely can and should think of your audience if you want to succeed in doing this work, *and you can absolutely, 100% manufacture a hit*.

Watching *Spinning Gold* proves that there are ways to reverse engineer what makes a "hit", according to Casablanca Records. All the artists they spotlight are bold, outspoken, larger-than-life personalities that stole every inch they were given and pushed for more.

They created categories and pushed them into the popular zeitgeist. Parliament pushed funk to the forefront. Donna Summers was the godmother of disco. KISS created hair metal and spectacle rock. The Isley Brothers stood at the bleeding edge of R&B.

Casablanca Records created categories. *That's how they manufactured hits.* They knew where the industry was, predicted where it was going, and saw the future.

Even in the movie, Neil Bogart basically says, "When I heard their music, I saw the future. All of it."

As a visionary-type leader myself, this is how I work, too, which is probably why it resonated with me that much.

Neil Bogart was a tastemaker. Casablanca Records led the industry into the future. *That was how they succeeded*. It's not the only way to succeed, but if they asked me to consult with them, I would tell them that across all their projects, they were trying to create the future.

Why weren't they successful in those first years?

For the same reason it took me forever to break through with non-fiction. The world wasn't ready for their sound, just like the publishing industry wasn't ready for direct sales in 2015. ***We were both living too far into the future.***

Casablanca was the living embodiment of Marty McFly.

That's why it made sense for them to pay DJs to play their records…because they needed to change the whole shape of the industry before people were comfortable buying their records.

This is not to say that everybody should build a "tastemaker" business. It is only to say that there is a definitive way to quantify what made Casablanca Records great.

No, not everything they made was successful, but knowing how they manufactured hits and staying in that zone of genius gives you the best chance at replicating that success…

…and avoiding their failures. If you aren't careful, the same thing that makes a visionary great is also what kills them in the end.

One of the hardest things for "tastemaker" artists to grapple with is that they don't always have to be "new". Somebody like Trent Reznor effectively created industrial rock, or at least broke it through to the masses, and then spent the next 30+ years refining it to what it is today.

He was a tastemaker who grew into an iconoclast. Most visionary artists spend their whole careers trying to be "new" instead of refining and honing what people love about their work.

Other writers work better acting as a warm, comfortable blanket. They create the same type of work every time, existing forever in the same space, writing the same kinds of stories, and relying on their fans to come back whenever they want the same "feeling" in their lives.

Their problem, of course, is that "comfort" artists can be drowned by the millions of others doing the same thing.

At their best, both of these creative types can learn and grow from each other.

As a visionary type, I learned to use my ability to "see the future" to create long-running series that take the best of where the industry was, what is popular at the moment, and where I envision the industry going and meld them into one product. Then, I combined that with the universal fantasy I give my readers and the themes that resonate through all my books to bring readers back to my work repeatedly.

That is how you manufacture a hit. It's not perfect, but it's way better than saying, "Just do your thing, buddy".

Telling people art is ephemeral and unquantifiable is wrong and unproductive to people trying to make art their lives. When the odds are stacked against you, empty platitudes won't help get you to the other side of the chasm.

That said, *there is some truth in Rubin's words because there are two parts to creating art:* building the scaffolding in pre-production and then crafting the piece into its finished form.

In the planning stage, you should absolutely be thinking about your audience because every decision you make at the world-building level will either expand or narrow your audience. *Are you making a broad fantasy starring a beautiful, tragic, relatable chosen one destined to save the world or a surrealist futuristic meditation on karma narrated by god?*

One of those two books will reach a broad audience and the other will be appreciated by a narrow one. ***Neither is wrong, but they define the audience.***

Considering your audience at this stage doesn't make your work more or less "authentic". It makes your art more or less marketable to a wide audience, but Taylor Swift makes work that is both authentic and broadly appealing.

More often than not, when I talk to authors, they are trying to market a niche book with a small potential audience like a book with a broad audience and mass market appeal.

No wonder they fail. You can't treat those two the same. Success looks different for each of them. You won't get the kind of CPC on the surrealist fiction to make Amazon ads profitable, for instance. So, you probably shouldn't do them.

Instead, you might focus on influencer marketing or building a niche audience mailing list that will pay top dollar and appreciate the quirkiness of it.

In general, the weirder your book, the more superfans will pay for it because there is nothing else like it. They scour the internet looking for similar books and are very appreciative when they find one.

The broader the appeal, the more people will buy it, but the more of a commodity it becomes because it looks like many other things.

Both books can be massively successful, but not if you are going into the production of a book with the wrong expectations. You have to figure out the marketability of your book before you write it.

I call this "putting on your publisher hat".

When you take that hat off and put on your "writer hat", you have to abandon all of that scaffolding and write for yourself because that is how you make something uniquely you that will resonate with your audience.

I have a 12-book series called *The Obsidian Spindle Saga,* and during pre-production for it, I decided to make it as broadly appealing as possible. The first book is called *The Sleeping Beauty* and features twists on fairy tales, mythology, and portal fantasy.

I made choices to make the series more appealing to more people. That said, the love story at the center of the story is between two women, which will limit the audience. Some people will love that part, while others will hate it, and still others will say that as a cis, het, white man, I don't have the right to center those kinds of stories.

In the planning stage, I understood all of that and still made those choices anyway. It was where my visionary self needed me to take the series so that I could remain interested throughout the process.

When I started writing the books, I took all that planning and added my unique twists to them. I wrote for just one person, my wife, and added specific elements I thought she would like into the story. I took all that planning and spun it in ways only I could make them fit together.

What came out was something nobody else in the world could have written, but it still had elements that would attract the broadest audience possible.

This is how commerce and art can work together in practice. I still made art. However, I made choices that expanded the audience beyond my earlier work.

No doubt using *The Sleeping Beauty, The Wicked Witch, The Fairy Queen,* and *The Red Rider* for the first four books will greatly increase the eyeballs willing to give the books a chance.

However, when readers interact with the series, it will be something only I could make because the words on the page were written without thinking about the broad audience at all.

A few years ago, I listened to a masterclass by Frank Gehry, and he talked about how he has the same constraints as everyone else. He has to deal with building codes, zoning, contracts, acoustics, and gravity. Because of that, 85% of his job is constrained, but it's in the last 15% that he has the freedom to do his art.

Artists think that constraints hamper them, ***but structure sets you and your audience free.*** You would never go on a rollercoaster if you weren't confident that you would survive the experience. Confidence in your survival is what allows you to experience fear in a safe and fun way.

In the same way, if your audience is not confident they understand the promise they will get with your book, they will not be able to fully experience your world and deal with their emotions in a safe way.

Additionally, you can't subvert tropes unless you understand those tropes. You can't break structure in ways that will delight your audience if you don't have a structure to begin with, either.

The more constraints you place on your work, the more your brain can explore and create true art. If you know the tropes of your genre and the brand promise you offer as an artist, you can break things in fun and interesting ways that will delight your readers.

Does structure destroy art, or does it enhance it? Does commerce degrade art, or does it allow for it to shine?

These are the questions artists have dealt with for generations, and there are no easy answers. What I do know is that I enjoy exchanging money for goods and services, but I also love creating art.

I have found ways to combine those things in ways that enhance both. Sometimes, I make a project for the widest audience and other times, I write books that will only appeal to my truest fans.

Both have value. However, knowing why I'm making a book and who I'm making it for helps determine a reasonable outcome for my art.

Most disappointment in art comes not from the creation of a piece but from the disparity between reality and expectation when art collides with commerce.

If we set realistic expectations, we can create better mental health practices for ourselves and sustain our careers for longer.

THE BULLSEYE METHOD FOR GROWING AN AUDIENCE

I write weird books. You might not believe me if you've come across me recently, but my first books included an epistolary novel told all in blog posts about a girl trying to prove her father's suicide was a murder so she doesn't leave her family home, a grounded sci-fi novel about a disabled boy who meets a homeless alien and has to help her get off the planet, a graphic novel I drew about a pickle that falls into a black hole and has to travel the universe to get back home, and a psychological horror dark fantasy comedy comic about a psychopath that doesn't know if they are killing people, monsters, or its all in their head the whole time.

Even if you are like, "All those sound amazing", you have to admit none of them are "center of the market" in the way that Deserts, or even Grasslands, think of the market. It's closest to how a Forest thinks about the market, but there were not even consistent themes in my work back then.

These books, along with *Anna and the Dark Place, The Void Calls Us Home, How NOT to Invade Earth*, and *Worst Thing in The Universe*, are what I consider my central canon. If you really love my work, you'll probably resonate with all these books, but they aren't likely to resonate with the "general audience".

Even my first non-fiction book, *How to Build Your Creative Career,* was originally called *Sell Your Soul: How to Build Your Creative Career.* It was a joke, a pun based around soul resonance selling, which is a term I started using a long time ago to talk about how to sell creative projects.

All of those books broke even at launch (*in fact, every book I've ever launched has*), but unless I was hand-selling the books to people, they didn't have much traction, and hand-selling a $20 book is really hard, especially ones as niche as what I wrote.

Then, everything changed with the introduction of *Katrina Hates the Dead.* Even though the story was still not "center of market", the artist went on to draw for Marvel, so there was a commercial style attached to it. People started picking up the book without me having to sell it, and that was nice.

Even nicer, people started to buy my other, weirder books, either in concert with their *Katrina Hates the Dead* purchase or after they finished it. This is where I developed The Bullseye Method.

The idea is that you have a core collection of books that are super weird and unsaleable to people because they are too off-market. Then, you create increasingly more commercial projects to drive people back to your core products.

My core books sit in the middle of everything I do. Those are the "superfan" books. I don't necessarily want them to be the first thing somebody reads when they come across my work, not because they aren't great, but because they are weird and might otherwise turn somebody off who would love my work.

Russell Nohelty

The Godsverse Chronicles is my second tier. I've done a lot of work to make this series more mainstream over the years as I expanded it from *Katrina Hates the Dead* and *Pixie Dust* into a 12-book series. This series deals with mythology, fairies, dragons, and everything that I love about fantasy, but it's an anthology series, which means you can read any book in any order. Even though the series is now much more marketable, when I first launched it, the series was way weirder. I actually added four books to the start of the series (*Magic, Evil, Time,* and *Heaven*) to ease people into the weirdness.

The Obsidian Spindle Saga is the next level up. It deals with everything in The Godsverse Chronicles but adds a lot of public domain characters and features titles like *The Sleeping Beauty, The Wicked Witch, The Fairy Queen,* and *The Red Rider* to hook people quickly and play on the ingrained nostalgia built into them. The other main thing this series has that sets it apart is that it centers on romance. It's not a romance, but the whole 12-book series is about this romance that will transcend time, space, and even the gods themselves. On top of being my best series, it's also the most commercial work I've ever put out in novel form.

Cthulhu is Hard to Spell expands even beyond that, though, because it wasn't written by me alone. It's an anthology series, which means I had dozens of creators helping me push it out. While Lovecraft's canon is not as popular as fairy tales, having so many amazing creators involved helped make this my most popular series ever.

But even better is that sales of *Ichabod Jones: Monster Hunter* exploded with the introduction of *Cthulhu is Hard to Spell*. Horror and fantasy fans suddenly had an easy way into my orbit, and many matriculated into my more avant-garde work.

This is true with my non-fiction, too. Earlier this year, I launched *This is NOT a Book, which is* clearly a core book for the audience I built up through my work with Monica and my other work. Even though it didn't do nearly as well as our *Direct Sales Mastery for Authors* book, it still made over $5,000 at launch, and people still matriculate there who want to explore the totality of my canon.

Even on this publication, I intentionally write easily consumable, SEO-friendly posts on occasion to attract the maximum number of new subscribers, some of whom will go on to read my more niche articles. I additionally release a serialized novel in my nonfiction publication because I know some percentage of readers will like both, and those are the ones I am most interested in delighting with my work. I am less interested in straight audience growth than I am in finding readers who will love everything I write from my books with wide appeal to my weird, niche books.

The beauty of this method is that as your audience expands, the floor of what you can make from your core books rises. Years ago, I launched *How NOT to Invade Earth* for 5 days, and made $3,420 on it. The next year, I launched the audio drama for *The Void Calls Us Home,* and it raised $4,618. The next year, I launched *Anna and the Dark Place,* and it raised $5,103. A few months ago, I launched my Wonderland duology, and it raised $5,357.

It's not an either/or for me. The broader stories support the core books, and I love them all. ***I have so much fun writing The Godsverse Chronicles***. I love working with so many creators on *Cthulhu is Hard to Spell*. I'm obsessed with The Obsidian Spindle Saga. They are my whole heart, just like my core books are, but there is intention behind them.

There is intention behind everything I do here, too. I write widely read posts people want to hear so that I can deliver weirder, niche pieces that people need to hear.

It's down at the core of everything I do. I live in Los Angeles, which has a long tradition of actors doing "one for the studio and one for me". That doesn't necessarily mean they love either role less. Sometimes, they do, but most of the time, they are indulging different parts of themselves with every story.

That resonates with me. Maybe it will resonate with you, too.

WILL THAT NEW SOCIAL MEDIA PLATFORM FUNDAMENTALLY IMPROVE YOUR EXISTENCE?

There is a very powerful sword belonging to a very powerful house in a very powerful *Franchise That Shall Not Be Named* that "only takes in that which makes it stronger".

I think about that idea a lot.

As a fantasy author, I spend much of my time thinking about the best magical powers, and aside from luck, which would be endlessly useful in just about any situation, it's hard for me to come up with a better power than the ability to discard that which does not serve you.

As a serial creative entrepreneur who is prone to shiny object syndrome, I have to work very hard to focus on that which will make me stronger and throw out the rest.

Even if something will serve me in the future, I am very careful about taking on things that will quickly fill my plate, as my plate is very small and prone to overflow.

Thus, when a new social media platform launches, my initial reaction is always, "Oh no".

I'm always eager to try new things, and a new social media platform is another game to play, which is appealing to my calculating brain. However, I know I cannot maintain a healthy relationship with social media.

Since I ended a very bad relationship with Facebook, I've scaled back my use of Twitter and Instagram so that I barely check them…

…but I'm a recovering validation slut. I need those little hearts and retweets like I need air.

Or at least that's my physiological response to it, even if my conscious mind knows that's not true.

Earlier this year, I watched *A Good Person*. While I have many feelings about whether Zach Braff will ever make a movie that holds together in even the most tenuous way, Florence Pugh was a delight as a junkie searching for help as she circles the drain into oblivion.

Delightful might be a weird way to describe a woman spiraling into the darkness of addiction, but I'm sticking with it. *She was incredible.* I truly felt her pain every moment she was on screen.

The thing I always connect with most in movies about addiction is when the addict realizes they will never be "cured". Addiction is a cycle that you can break but never be rid of completely. It is always there, in the back of your brain, waiting to strike…

…and if you aren't careful, it will tell you, "Maybe a little wouldn't hurt" in your weakest moment, urging you to pick up that phone again.

In your weakest moment, you will believe your lizard brain and the cycle will start again. It doesn't matter if you've been clean for a week or a decade; that's the work.

Even now, while I'm writing about being addicted to social media, I am wondering what is happening over on Notes. My fingers even twitched for a second there, thinking about it.

There is no doubt that I've met some amazing people on social media, but it's hard to separate that from the fact that the platforms are fundamentally run by Silicon Valley entrepreneurs and funded by venture capital.

Those investors want the founders to take their money and turn it into more money by squeezing the lifeblood out of its users.

If an investor expects a 25% ROI, that means the company has to grow considerably more than that year-over-year to generate enough money to make the VC business model work.

If you want to know the underlying reason Cory Doctorow coined the enshittification of social media, it all comes down to this kind of thing. Social media companies are incentivized to raise money from venture capital to pay for marketing and growth. To entice creators, they make the platforms fun and make it easy to engage with your fans. Then, they pull the rug out from under you when you rely on the platform most.

This is the perverse set of benchmarks VC-backed companies are placed under when they take investment money. To create value, they need users. So, they trick you into using their terrible platform by temporarily making it seem not terrible for a time.

It happened to Facebook. It happened to Instagram. It happened to Twitter (even in the pre-Musk days). It's already starting to happen to TikTok. It will happen to Threads, too, and everything that comes after it because that's how enshittification works.

When one platform, like Facebook, succeeds, it has to support the entire industry by squeezing every dollar out of its users.

The thing with venture capital is that it doesn't want you to be happy. Capitalism wants you to be depressed. Heck, it's probably causing your depression.

Capitalism does not present good options. At best, it presents fewer bad options and allows you to choose what part of your soul you want to betray to stay alive.

Yes, there is "choice", but they are all bad ones. It just depends on what kind of bad you are able to tolerate without completely dying inside. ***It's depressing, and that's the point.***

People are better capitalist consumers when they are depressed. Depression breaks down your willpower. It zaps your strength. It makes you more likely to click those precious ads that feed the gears of capitalism.

Social media is one of the best delivery devices capitalism ever invented because it bombards you with a nonstop barrage of other people's best moments while making you believe that your next purchase will solve all your problems.

If you wonder why social media makes you feel terrible, it is a feature of the system, not a bug.

There is no profit in happiness ; thus, it has no value in capitalism. That without value must be cast aside so the gaping maw of capitalism can be fed in perpetuity. Capitalism will always eat that which feeds it until it starves. I just wasn't ready for it to happen so soon after I kicked the habit of social media.

So, of course, I relapsed. Three months after Facebook disappeared me, I decided to try again. *How bad could it be, right?* If Facebook were a person, what happened to me would be considered emotional abuse, but for a social media platform, it was a normal Monday.

Still, as I mentioned before, *I'm a social media addict.* Just because I was "sober" for months didn't change that fact. Unfortunately, one of the biggest truths about addiction is that people who recover often think they can take just a little taste, which brings them back into the addiction cycle again.

I decided to come back a little bit. I created a burner account, and I figured, how bad could it be to accept friend requests from people? Hundreds were waiting for me at that point.

So, I did, but I carefully unfollowed every person I friended so I wouldn't see them in my news feed.

It turned out that wasn't so bad. In fact, I started getting some DMs from old friends, and that was nice. So, I thought, how bad could it be to join some of my favorite groups? At first, I unfollowed even the groups, but then I started to follow them again, which led to me seeing posts and commenting, which led to panic attacks when people would reply asking follow-up questions or disagreeing with me.

I had rolling panic attacks all that week. This is not a medical term since there is little scholarship behind having a panic attack for a week straight, but I know my body. Basically, from Monday to Friday, when I shut off my account again, I was in a constant state of panic and agitation.

It wasn't until I talked about this with my business partner late Friday night that I realized what was happening. *This was how I used to feel all the time,* keyed up with every interaction. It wasn't until I cut the addiction off and returned to it that I realized what was happening.

The same thing happened when I returned to doing shows. It took me less than a week to fall back into the old habits that made me feel terrible for years. So, I unfollowed almost all my groups. I will still keep getting DMs from friends because I like that part. Otherwise, I have to make a clean break for my mental health.

Is there any hope in this hypercapitalist dystopia? *Nebulously, but that's about all you can hope for these days.*

There is good news, though. *You can still make money without succumbing to the capitalist meat grinder.* The exchange of money for goods and services is not the problem most people have with capitalism. This exchange isn't even capitalism; it's commerce, and we've already talked about the big difference between the two.

While we're talking about how VC firms use capitalism to keep you addicted to feeling terrible so that you buy all the things, we should probably discuss the value of a social media follower to your author business compared to the value of an email subscriber. Since we're forced to live in a hypercapitalist hellscape, we might as well try to use it to our advantage, right?

The value of a newsletter subscriber is generally agreed by many to be around $40. However, that is variable based on many factors.

By another calculation, an email subscriber is worth $1/mo, or $12/yr, though others argue that metric should really be $1/mo for everyone who opens your email.

Last year, I could track almost all of the $184,459.41 I made (in revenue, not profit) to my 25,000-person email lists, even though I didn't have a subscription at all because I launched ten books and multiple courses.

One important thing to note is that fiction newsletters often have to be bigger than nonfiction ones to get the same results since nonfiction email lists can offer courses, coaching, and more to their subscribers. I have a friend who runs a seven-figure business from a 6,000-person email list. Meanwhile, my fiction friends generally need a list of at least 20,000 people, plus they need to invest in massive ad spends to get the same results.

Meanwhile, the value of your whole Facebook author page is something like $60 to Facebook's valuation.

Of course, that is an average cost across every page. Within that, each page has a different value based on the follower count and engagement. I can tell you that before I lost my Facebook account, I had 15,000 fans on my page, which equated to about $1,000 a year in sales. That would make a follower worth roughly $.06.

However, this is not the only way you can monetize your social media accounts. Influencers can use their account to book sponsored advertising. How much could they make? According to Shopify, this is how much you can charge depending on your account size:

- **Micro influencers (10,000 - 50,000 followers):** $100 - $500 per post.
- **Mid-tier influencers (50,000 - 500,000 followers):** $500 - $5,000 per post.
- **Macro influencers (500,000 - 1,000,000 followers):** $5000 - $10,000 per post.
- **Mega influencers (1,000,000+ followers):** $10,000+

From that pricing, it seems like 10,000 followers are worth $100 to a brand or $.01 per post.

If you could book one promotion a day that would be $36,500, or the value would be $3.65 per year in value. We all know you can't book that many promoted posts, but that's the highest value.

So, a Facebook follower is worth somewhere between $.06/yr and $3.65/yr, depending on how you use your account. That said, if you don't have at least 10,000 followers, it's nearly impossible to book these types of promotions.

Every social media platform has a different worth that shifts over time, but as you weigh your decision about going all-in on a new platform, it's important to look soberly at those statistics.

Above just the ROI, you need to weigh whether you want to "build your castle in somebody else's sandbox" and pour time into a platform where you don't own the customer data. If the story of my Facebook account getting locked shows nothing else, it should show that a social media platform can be taken away from you in an instant, either by malice, stupidity, or simply by changing the algorithm to make it harder to connect with your followers. ***Then, the worth of your account drops to zero in an instant.***

For me, the math isn't worth it. On top of that, followers usually lock you into a platform because you can't take them with you if you leave (Fediverse social media sites like Mastadon and BlueSky notwithstanding).

It's great for the platform because it ties us deeper into the platform, but it's just another hook to keep you locked into an environment. It's a subtle, gentle hook, but a hook nonetheless.

When we own the chain of custody for our subscribers, platforms lose. They only gain significant value when they control the data and can dole it out as they see fit. If we can take our subscribers and leave the platform without repercussions, their stock value won't go up.

It's the same reason why publishers try to grab as many rights as possible for as long as possible. Their value is in the size of the horde they collect.

The value is not in the size of a platform. It's in how much of it a company owns, and they want to own it all.

This is a dangerous precedent for Substack and, sadly, sends it further down the road of every social media platform that came before it.

So, ask yourself this question. Do you really want to sign up for a new social media app, or are you searching for the transformation you hope will come from a new social media app and how it could change your life circumstances?

This is the question at the heart of joining any new platform for me. I am not looking for a new social media app. I don't really care about social media. If I joined, I would only be searching for the transformation that a new social media app promises.

What is that transformation for you?

If you're a Grassland, you're probably looking to be known as a thought leader. If you're a Forest, you're probably looking to connect with a group of fans who adore your quirky, unique voice. If you're a Tundra or Aquatic, you're probably looking to tap into your fandom to build excitement for a launch or expand into new formats.

But are there other ways to get that same result without social media? There probably are. My articles get read by 10,000+ people. I can't imagine more than that number saw my posts on social media.

Will a new platform actually make you the person you want to be? That is the fantasy social media is selling. They sell you the dream of having an audience clamor for your every word and let you live the life you have envisioned for years.

There is so much FOMO in not joining that we tell ourselves this is the one that will change everything, so we can't sit out.

Is that realistic, though? How many people will actually win that lottery? Not many. People talk about the "glory days" of social media when the internet was better, but I don't think those days ever really existed.

What I do think existed were moments when "social media salons" formed.

If you don't know about salons, they were moments in time when the conditions were such that great minds converged in a singular place and created a community together. Silicon Valley in the 80s was one of them. Paris in the 20s was another.

I believe the same thing happened on social media.

At a certain time and place on the internet, people found their "salons" where the conditions were just right, and they caught the pocket perfectly to find a wholesome community that fed them.

I don't think any social media platform was ever good. *I will die on that hill.* However, I do think that in certain moments, the right collection of people gathered in a singular place and created magic.

Whether you found that on Twitter, Instagram, or wherever, it's okay to mourn it…but it likely is gone.

You can go to Paris today, but it's not like being there at the peak of Hemingway's era when the greatest writers of the day all gathered in a single cafe.

I feel like Substack has become that place for me. I found it on Kickstarter in the mid-2010s. I have been very lucky to find it multiple times in my life, and I cherish it, but I also know it won't be there forever.

Eventually, the conditions change, and salons break up into the wind. They don't last forever, and they can never be recreated, no matter how hard you try.

If you actually want a new social media app for whatever reason people care about with new social media apps, then you should go for it.

Social media is genuinely exciting to Deserts. There are optimizations to find, codes to crack, and games to win. If you are a Desert, a new social media platform probably feels like a boon to your business. If you aren't a Desert, you should find one to be your social media manager.

For other ecosystems, there are usually more negatives than positives with social media unless you win the game.

Do you want scale or do you want security? When I dig deep with authors, most of them don't have any interest in virality or scaling. What they want is to be secure in the knowledge that when they release something, an audience will buy from them and adoringly read their work.

They want to know that they can pay their mortgage next month. Moreover, they want to know they'll be able to do this work for the next year and many years down the road.

There are some people who genuinely want virality and to be a personality, but if you don't care about that, I would ask whether you want that movie deal or the ability to spend two years focused on your work with the money that comes from it.

Do you really want 100,000 followers, or do you want the $50-$100k in stable income every year that possibly comes with that kind of following?

Do you want a big following, or do you want to do the work you care about for an audience that matters?

Those are two very different things. They are interconnected, but you can build a great business with a relatively small following.

Most authors hate the social media game and despise the performative machinations social media forces on them. It is worth it if they win, but they rarely win, and then it becomes a burden.

If you're looking at social media as simply a means to an end, then ask yourself if/how other social media sites have actually helped you reach that end.

Can this new social media app actually accomplish your stated goal? Is it worth the trouble to find out? Will it light you up more than it will drain you?

Most importantly, are there better ways to get that without leveraging a new social platform?

Because there is a big opportunity cost in investing in a social media platform, even for a short time. There is a mental load cost and a sunk cost in spending your time trying to get traction somewhere. There is an even bigger one with failing and picking yourself up off the floor.

Maybe you finish this thought exercise and say, "Yes, it's still worth it", and that's fab.

However, if you're still on the fence, I would question whether your previous efforts were worth it and whether there's a better way for you to spend your time instead of being a statistic to boost a company's stock price.

Very few people can win the viral game. Yes, BookTok helped inject millions into the publishing industry last year, but that power was vastly concentrated in very few titles.

Colleen Hoover won. ***She deserves everything.*** However, since then, she has been used as a model for other authors, "encouraging" them to use TikTok because there's money there. I use that term loosely because it's usually more like guilting or cajoling or, at best, flippantly replying to a heartfelt plea for help with advice to try this new, shiny thing to fill the darkness in your soul.

Whenever I see that type of thing, I remember that most people who won the gold rush were selling pickaxes and maps. Levi's won the gold rush.

There are a million sustainable paths to build your author career that can fulfill you, but every way I know how to make money is boring.

Almost every way successful authors make money is boring. Even people who go viral usually don't sustain it for long. Even viral stars build boring companies. They build marketing companies, sell physical goods, or become advertising brands. Some become angel investors. Yes, they also make money with their videos, but they usually get rich doing something boring.

Social media promises excitement, but excitement is a very small part of a sustainable business, even for a Tundra, who monetizes excitement best among all the ecosystems.

If you love social media and/or get something from it, awesome, but if you are doing it for the money instead of the lolz, then there probably *ain't money in them there hills* for you.

That said, you might strike it rich just by trying. A few people did so during the gold rush days, and they were immediately used as examples to get other people to buy in and keep the money flowing.

If that doesn't sound great to you, though, maybe instead of chasing social media fame, pour that energy into writing a new book, learning advertising, or figuring out what marketing will work for you that fills you up instead of drains you.

Even if it is good now, will it really be good for long? For some of us, the answer is yes, but is it a yes for you?

Social media networks sell a dream. They tell you that you will be happy on this platform, that this platform will solve your problems, and that it will turn you into the person you always wanted to be.

But nothing is a simple bullet to that dream, and I'm sick of being fed a dream. I would rather plant somewhere and make the dream come true in a place that feels good to me.

OBJECTIVELY GOOD AND SUBJECTIVELY YOUR JAM

People often ask me how I get over bad reviews and keep going even when people are unimaginably cruel. I have a strategy for it, but I think it's important to note that my initial, visceral reaction to bad reviews is still…well, bad.

I do have a secret weapon, though…

…data.

That's right. The thing most writers opine as the bane of their existence is my savior.

I've given enough talks where one person ranked me as a 10 and another marked me as a 7 for the *exact* same metric based on the *exact* same content that I have come to grips with the only reasonable conclusion…*reviews are subjective.*

It's to the point where I stare at the review sheet wondering what presentation certain people were watching when I see the final numbers. But their feelings are valid, so I swallow it and move on.

I've seen enough people yell at me for an email while others praise me for the same words that it's hard to take either with much rigor. These are two emails I received 30 minutes apart from two different humans. The text of the email was EXACTLY the same, and yet the responses were night and day.

How can you look at this and think anything except the universe is utter, nonsensical chaos?

I've watched enough people bash things I love and adore things I hate to believe it's any more than vibes. Still, I'm a data nerd at heart with a degree in sociology, so I started to think about it and realized there's an easy explanation for why these types of things happen.

It turns out things can be measured on two metrics, objective goodness and subjective goodness, and we're only taught to consider the latter.

Objectively good: Something meets the minimum standards of a medium. If your building doesn't fall down, doesn't kill people, and has doors, rooms, windows, floors, and a roof, along with necessary appliances…it is probably objectively good. Something that "meets spec" is objectively good. If your book reads well, is well-formatted, has a well-designed cover, and doesn't break apart when you pick it up, it's probably reached a level of objective goodness. This metric is something we can judge and rate, but only pass/fail.

Subjective goodness: Do you actually like the prose? Does the story resonate with you? Is the building aesthetically pleasing to you? Are you moved by a piece of work? These are measures of subjective good, and almost all metrics of "good" are about subjective goodness because things that aren't objectively good aren't even finished.

My wife doesn't agree with me on this, but I'm 100% sure that every industry has a degree of objective goodness baked inside of it. College, in many ways, can be seen as a way to impart objective goodness to students, which they can use as benchmarks in their careers.

If your work is ***objectively bad***, that's a you problem. If your work is ***objectively good*** and ***subjectively*** not somebody's jam, that's a them problem, not a you problem.

It becomes a you problem when you have to market and sell your work, but if somebody reads something and doesn't resonate with it, then there's nothing you can do about it. All you have control over is the work you create, not what somebody thinks of it.

The more niche your work, the fewer people will think it is subjectively good. We are never taught the difference between objective and subjective good, though, so almost everyone trashes something objectively good even though it is only subjectively not their jam.

As a writer, it's really important to understand this distinction. I do not like *Game of Thrones*, but I do appreciate the objective goodness and quality of it. *Diary of a Teenage Girl* by Phoebe Gloeckner is a brilliant book. I am uncomfortable reading it, but I appreciate it for the artful way it was constructed.

As writers, we must be able to analyze things we don't like for their objective ***and*** subjective quality. It's one of the most important ways to improve your work. If you cannot zoom out and notice the quality of a work, you will never grow beyond what you already know.

If you want more people to think your work is subjectively good, then you should learn how to create onramps to more groups so that it resonates with more people or find platforms where your type of work already resonates.

You can control making something objectively good or even a commentary of objective goodness. You cannot control whether something is subjectively somebody's jam. You can work at making a piece of work convey the meaning you intend, but people still have to work to find that meaning.

Almost everything, though, will not be somebody's jam any more than everything is your jam. If you can notice the way you resonate and reject these things in your own life, it can help you see this same impulse in others.

GROWTH, OR SOMETHING LIKE IT

There is a darkness that comes with growth.

It's as if you are consumed inside an abyss because there is no light to guide you.

This is because you have not set a beacon yet. Once you have figured out the path to get what you want, your mind places a little light there. Every time you return, the light gets a little brighter until it is as bright as the sun.

However, in those moments of growth, when you haven't reached your destination, you are in the dark. Your little flashlight can not see more than a foot in front of you.

It's scary, and even if you have a guide, that doesn't make it much better. There is no way to stop the darkness from encroaching on you. All you can do is prepare for it.

You still have to go into the darkness. Others can tell you the path, but you have to walk it. You still have to set your beacon.

Once you do, it will become easier and easier to go there again.

And then you will be off into the darkness again to set a new beacon.

Most people cannot deal with the darkness of growth. They stay by their existing beacons and never venture forward into the darkness.

They have heard stories of the darkness being unforgiving and all-consuming, and it is, but once you come to know the darkness, there is a comfort to it as well.

The darkness is what leads to growth, and though it is cold and foreboding, you also know it is necessary to get where you are going.

You are brave for venturing into the darkness. Most people never do. You are an explorer. You are trying, and that is more than most people will ever do. Then, when you reach the other side, you can light a beacon for others.

That beacon you place is the brand that allows people to find you.

Unfortunately, they still have to walk the path, too, and no matter how much you help, it's scary to step foot into the darkness and forge your own path.

Many people ask me why I'm so concerned with people monetizing their work. While I appreciate lots of people just want to write, what I have seen again and again is that, eventually, if you don't make money on something, you will burn out at it.

Heck, you might burn out if you do make money on something, but you are sure to do so if you don't.

This is because passions are often hard and expensive, and lying in bed surrounded by books is easy. It's much easier to zone out and play video games than to do the hard work of this blog, my podcast, or even writing books.

My podcast, The Complete Creative, ran for 200 episodes and made me a total of $100. I loved that podcast, but eventually, it became impossible to put in the resources required to make it better because it wasn't making any money.

I couldn't pay for advertising, and I couldn't pay for a better editor. I couldn't do anything to make it better.

Since I couldn't improve on it, the show stagnated and became boring.

I've met so many people who had to abandon their dreams because they couldn't grow it effectively. Either they didn't have the money or audience to make it worthwhile.

So, they gave up. Maybe they didn't abandon their dream entirely, but it became a hobby they only did sporadically when they had time and no longer shared it widely with the world.

Yes, some people took it up as a hobby and then got a job, but most people just abandoned the thing they loved because it became too hard to push that boulder up a hill with no reward.

There are only so many hours in a day, and it's hard to spend the few free hours people have on something that costs a lot of money and doesn't grow at all.

However, when you see growth in something, it becomes easy to invest more time and money into it because all your hard work is paying off.

This is why I think it's so important to learn the marketing side of things; you will see growth in your business and invest more in it. Then, there will be more cool things in the world, and I can buy them all.

Even if you make no money, you will at least find more people to appreciate your work. Many creators say they don't care about the money. I have never met anyone who didn't want to find more people who resonated with their message.

Somebody asked me on a podcast once what the difference was between marketing and sales. I have always had a hard time explaining it quickly, but this time, I had an answer I didn't want to forget.

Sales generate immediate revenue, whether that's Kickstarter, book sales, or launching a course through a sales page. ***Sales initiatives drive direct sales and are all about immediate ROI.***

Marketing is brand awareness that drives down the cost of acquiring future sales. This might be guest blogging, hopping on a podcast, doing a strategic partnership, or even certain ad buys that don't lead to a sales page. Sales from marketing come indirectly.

The more people know, like, and trust your brand, the less you will have to convince them to buy your next product, and you can convert them to sales much more quickly and cheaply.

Russell Brunson once talked about how producing a single marketing video reduced his cost per registration from $150 to $50. Even though that video wasn't selling anything specific, it was so ubiquitous and did such a good job explaining the company that it cut the cost of ads by 66%.

That's good marketing.

Interestingly, sales campaigns like Kickstarter have marketing and brand awareness built into them. You get marketing while you're making sales, but you do not necessarily get sales by doing marketing.

The question for sales campaigns is, "Will this give me an immediate ROI?"

However, for marketing campaigns, the question might be best summarized as, "Will enough of my ideal customers engage with this effort, and will it lower the acquisition costs for my next launch enough to make it worth it for me to participate?"

Both are important, but they serve different functions.

So many people I know say they want a bigger following, more readers, more sales, etc. However, I never see them do anything to attract new fans except posting to their social media walls. They do no marketing. They do no advertising. They do very few shows or promotions of any kind.

I have no idea how I would get more people to read my work without constant marketing and advertising.

I drive an average of 1,000 new subscribers a month to my mailing list, and I still barely feel like I'm getting ahead most days. Before I did that, I was doing 30-40 shows a year. Before that...well, before that, I had a very small audience that didn't ever grow.

How does somebody who doesn't do any of that stuff expect to build a following and sustain themselves?

Word of mouth?

Magic?

I am very curious about this because I am constantly trying new things, working new angles, and working to increase my marketing. Every time I think that my business needs a shot in the arm, I do some promotion to drive in new fans.

I don't know how I would survive without doing those things and making sure new people are always finding my work. I know I would never have been able to grow so fast. I would likely still be where I was four years ago, without any fans, barely able to survive.

The minute I figured out marketing, even a little bit, was the day everything else unlocked for me. There is nothing wrong with speaking to a small audience, but if you want to grow fast, you need a marketing plan, too.

The #1 question I get asked about marketing is, "How can I do more with less?". There are some amazing ways to extend your marketing calendar, cross-promote with other people, and expand your reach without overextending yourself.

- **Repurposing previously written articles—**You can do a "season of reruns" or a "season of updates" where you take your old posts and either beef them up with new information or comment on them with how things have changed in some way.
- **Repurposing things you said on social media—** Take posts you've made and comment on them, comment on posts other people have made, or make your posts articles you send to your audience.
- **Voicemails—**Either record voicemails for your subscribers or get voicemails from them and do a roundup of them.

- **Best of lists**—This can be compiled by somebody else, like a VA or even AI, if you give them the format. You can also pull a bunch of quotes about a subject and line them
up. Resilience, Courage, Love, whatever you want. This is also a great way to build SEO with your target audience.
- **Q and A**—If you do take voicemails, you can use them as a Q and A segment where the audience is making most of the content except for your answer.
- **Hire a "monthly intern" or "guest editor"**—Rusty Foster from Today in Tabs hires monthly interns, and Monica and I were guest editors on an issue of Indie Author Magazine.
- **Asynchronous interviews**—Lots of people do asynchronous interviews, where you send a series of similar questions to people and then post their responses.
- **Cross-posting**—One of the easiest things you can do is to cross-post interesting articles (with permission) to your audience.
- **Guest posting**—This takes longer if you're the one writing it, but it's an amazing way to get more content, especially if you have a publication with some traction.

Some of the above strategies can be implemented by yourself, but most are only powerful when you work with other people. I am very high on Connectedness on CliftonStrengths, so I love working with other people.

That said, it does require putting yourself out there and sometimes dealing with rejection, so I want to offer a caveat. It's okay, and even good, to support other people, even if they are doing a similar thing as you…

…but it's not required, and **nobody** has the right to expect your support if you don't want to give it.

As good as it feels to support things you care about, it feels equally gross to be guilted into supporting something you don't enthusiastically support.

"Support" is a really convenient cudgel of manipulative people. It makes you *feel* like a jerk, but really, **they** are the jerk.

They know decorum and societal norms will push against you until you give in so you don't come across as a **squeaky wheel.**

It's subtle, but it's still manipulation, and those kinds of people can screw all the off.

There is nothing wrong in the asking, but there is something **very wrong** in the guilting.

You can always tell what kind of human you're dealing with after you politely decline to promote their work.

Good people are gracious. Bad people become vicious.

If their response to your decline is anything short of "*No worries. Thanks for taking the time to think about it*", you should be very skeptical of every word out of their mouth.

Promotion is a gift, not a requirement.

You don't have the right to it. You don't automatically get it with every project. Even if you've gotten it before, it doesn't mean you will get it next time.

If something isn't given freely, then it shouldn't be taken by force, and guilt is a type of force.

Relationships are not transactional. They are cooperative, and cooperation is symbiotic. If one person is manipulating the other, then that is parasitic.

We don't nurture parasites. We kill them with fire.

Stop trying to use "supporting each other" to guilt people into promoting you.

It's gross, and we all see you. A perfectly acceptable response to somebody asking you to do something is:

"I can't do that"

Do not let people tell you otherwise. They will heap things on you until you break. No, past the time you break, while you are crawling along the floor battered and unable to move.

They won't even notice your misery.

They will take. Always. Do not let them. If you can't do something, or even if you don't want to do something, you have to understand it's okay to say no.

They will play every card to get you to do it anyway, but you have every right to say no.

I was at a party recently, and I could not have been more uncomfortable. The party was loud, and I didn't know many people. It was the kind of place 21-year-old Russell would have gone to, but 36-year-old Russell felt out of place.

There was absolutely nothing wrong with the place I was at, either. The other people that were there seemed to be having a perfectly pleasant time. It was the right place for them, but I could not have been more awkward and ill at ease because it wasn't the right place for me.

I may have said 100 words the whole night, which, if you know me, is not normal.

However, it made me realize that often, there is nothing wrong with us when we're trying to connect with our audience. We are just in the wrong place, talking to the wrong people, surrounded by the wrong music, dancing to the wrong beat.

In another setting, I'm perfectly pleasant.

In the right setting, you would have to pay me to shut up. In fact, just a few weeks ago, I was with many of the same people and had a perfectly lovely time chatting up a storm. However, when I'm in the wrong setting, I don't have the energy. It's the same for us in our creative lives.

Often, it's not that there's anything wrong with us. It's just that we're out of place. When we find the right place, we'll shine. All of this stuff we're doing is to find our people.

The easiest way to find the right buyers is to search for buyers who are already performing the action you want them to take.

If you want more people to buy from you at conventions, go to conventions and find buyers there. If you want people to buy on Kickstarter, find buyers who already use Kickstarter. If you want people to buy on Amazon...well, you get the idea.

So many people I meet are trying to convince their existing fans to buy things in a completely different way.

And while that might work, generally, people have buying patterns that are baked into them from years of habitual use.

I have people who will buy anything I put on a table at a show, but they will NEVER buy a Kickstarter. I have people who will back a Kickstarter but won't buy a book on Amazon.

And so on.

We all have our habits, and it's hard to break them. You will never get me to start a pull list in a store or buy floppy comics in general.

I generally buy my books on Kickstarter, at shows, or I buy ebooks on Amazon.

Now, if you put your books there, you have the best shot to earn my business quickly.

Will I go and buy your book another way? Maybe, in time, but it certainly won't be fast because I'm already attuned to the way those systems work.

So, instead of finding people and trying to convert them into the kind of buyers you want them to be...

...what if you just went out and found new buyers who acted the way you already wanted and convinced them your book was cool, too?

If somebody already buys lots of fantasy novels on Nook, and you want people to buy your fantasy novel on Nook, all you have to do is convince them your book is cool instead of convincing them to change their buying habits.

The only time I change buying habits is when I shift businesses. The minute I started writing ebooks in earnest, I started buying tons of books on Amazon and other platforms.

But I only started doing that *because it was easy and beneficial to me.*

If it weren't, I would keep buying books on Kickstarter and shows, like I always have before.

If it's working for you, great, but if you are having trouble finding buyers to act the way you want them to act, find buyers who already act the way you want them to act and try to make them know, like, and trust you.

Once you know how people buy and what they like, all you have to do is convince them to like you. If you can convince other people to like you, you can convince those new people to like your work, too. It just takes effort.

Everybody is a fan of something already. Your goal is to make somebody from being a fan of something else into a fan of your work. One of the most common methods to make this happen is something I call "The Switch", and it's remarkably effective if you do it the right way.

The idea is simple.

If somebody likes X and your work is like X, then a person has a very good chance of also liking your work, which we'll call Y. However, they've had years to build up their love for X, and they have no idea who you are or why they should care about you or Y.

The problem is creators often find people who like X and assume they are ready to enjoy their Y, so they immediately whack them over the head with their Y without giving people who like X a reason why they should care about Y first.

Giving them a reason why is critical for The Switch to work.

The Switch is all about taking fans from X to Y, but by way of U, or, more accurately, *by way of liking you first.* The secret ingredient in The Switch is that potential fans start to like you before they like your work. If you can take somebody from liking X to liking you, then they will be highly likely to try your Y.

Why is that?

Because you are giving them a reason why they should like your work which is deeper than, "You like X, so logically, you will like Y." Instead, you are saying, "Hey, you like me, and you like X. You should try Y because I think you will like it due to Z reasons."

When people like you, they are way more likely to try anything you offer them. This is because they've built empathy with you like they would with a friend. Since you know they like X, once they try your work, they will likely love it, too.

The Switch is all about wedging yourself between somebody else's work and your own work and creating empathy between them and you.

Almost everybody misses that middle point and forgets that the easiest way to get people to like your work is to get them to like you. Once you have refined this process, you can start plugging in new people from different existing fandoms and watch your fanbase soar.

It's unfair to expect somebody to buy from you the first time they see your work, isn't it?

I mean, here you are, a perfect stranger, talking to another perfect stranger and trying to convince them you are a good use of their finite resources in just a couple of minutes.

That's a bonkers expectation, right? I mean, most people won't do that.

Sometimes, I do it, and sometimes, people do it to me, but usually, people need to know me for a while before they buy from me, and that seems normal for me as well. This is a work where a lot of people are trying to trick you out of your money, and our money is finite. It takes a lot to pry it out of my hands.

Are there ways to convince the right people to buy right away? Sure, and you should learn them. It often works for me to have people buy all at once, but when it doesn't, I don't feel bad about it because that's normal. People generally need to know you for a while before they are going to feel comfortable spending money on your work.

There are so many ways to spend money nowadays that it's becoming even harder for people to part with their money on the first interaction. Usually, it will take 7-14 interactions, or touchpoints, before somebody gets comfortable with you.

The more expensive it is, the more they will need to know you and the more touchpoints you will need to get them to trust you. Don't treat this as a failure. Treat it as an opportunity. If you can make them understand that you are amazing, then they'll buy from you later.

Your business is not a short-term play. Yes, we need money right now, but we also need money in a year, two years, and ten years from now, and the more people you can bring into your ecosystem and show that you are awesome, the more who will get comfortable enough to buy from you in the future, and future you will appreciate it when they do.

I am willing to give almost anything away for free because then people come into my mailing list, where I then try to sell them other things.

Once you have that mechanic, the more people you hook, the better the sales funnel gets.

The problem is this...you can't do it a little bit, really, at least what I'm doing. I'm trying to be everywhere all at once. I need to be seen everywhere because once everyone is talking about me, word of mouth spreads quickly, and my notoriety goes up. I was very, very strategic about this when I came to substack hard in May. I wanted to be everywhere and be connected to everyone of note in my ideal audience's life.

With fiction, well, take the *One Damned Good Thing Kickstarter.* I cross-promoted with five other campaigns in the same universe and then did promotional swaps with 20 more creators during my campaign because I needed buyers to see my campaign a bunch of times and associate me with quality.

Once they associate me with quality and associate me with a creator they already know and like, then they eventually buy.

But I have a system that works. I know exactly how people become buyers of my work, and I know the actions I have to take to make that happen.

You don't have that stuff, though, it seems like, which makes it harder.

There is a reason I write 5,000+ posts every week. It's because almost nobody else can do it as well or as long as I do. Others might start, but I've been doing it for years at this point, and I know that I'll keep doing it. I also know they can't keep up. It's too hard a bar to summit continuously.

It's an action that sets me apart from other people. If you want that kind of thing, you have to come to me because nobody does it better.

Then, I also speak at conferences, host live streams, and guest on podcasts to get people into my universe because I know a fractional share will convert.

The problem is, for most people, the fractional share they get is almost non-existent once their potential readers finish moving through their funnel. For me, it's not. For me, it's quite a bit, and I have the mechanic to turn those eyeballs into sales.

So, yeah. I'll give it almost all away because I know I have so much more for people to find and pay for.

I used to think I didn't want to email my list too much because it would bother them.

Then, I started to hear from people whose lists I was on that they didn't want to email too much, and I almost reached through the internet and shook them in frustration.

When I sign up for a list, I want to hear from people when they have cool things to share.

As long as you are sharing cool things with me, then you can email me 5x a day for all I care (*but probably 1x a day is a good upper limit*).

It's only if you don't have cool things to share that I don't want to hear from you, and if you don't think it's cool, why are you writing it in the first place?

The only time I'll unsubscribe from you is if you stop sharing things that resonate with me, and I'll do that whether you email me once a month or once a day.

People always say, "I don't want to get too many emails", but what they really mean is, "I don't want to get too many *garbage* emails".

If you don't think what you're writing is garbage, then it's not a garbage email, so send it.

If you think it's garbage, don't write it.

How can you tell? If you can't think of a unique purpose that your email serves, it's probably garbage. If it doesn't shed new light on something in any way, then it's probably garbage. If readers learn nothing new from it, it's probably garbage.

If you are providing new information to people who have signed up to hear that information, whether it's about a book launch or a new article, it's probably not garbage.

A not insignificant part of my business is doing book marketing for authors. The vast majority of this work comes in the form of giveaways that I run through Booksweeps.

These giveaways are heavily targeted to specific fandoms, like Supernatural, Buffy, Harry Potter, etc.

I am exceedingly good at this form of marketing, but this is a story of a pretty big mistake I made a few years ago.

Because I have run so many of these giveaways, I usually start the ad process by cloning a previously successful campaign and then tweaking the targeting. For instance, in 2017, I ran a campaign for *Harry Potter*, which collected over 7,000 new emails in 10 days.

When I eventually ran a giveaway targeted at *Supernatural* fans, I duplicated that ad campaign and tweaked the targeting from *Harry Potter* fans to *Supernatural* fans, along with tweaking the ad copy and images.

It's very important to do all three of those things because otherwise, you will be targeting the wrong fans with the wrong imagery, thus increasing your cost per click and throwing off your whole campaign.

The above is important to understand for reasons I will now explain.

Once upon a time, I was running a giveaway for *Legend of Zelda*. As I always do, I cloned a previously successful campaign, this time Supernatural, to do my targeting.

I checked the images and ad copy, and then I started the ad set.

Before any giveaway officially starts, I always take some time to run tests. This is to make sure everything is working well with a fairly small portion of the overall ad budget before I increase the spend to its normal level.

Thank god I do it, too, because this time, during testing, I started to notice that many people who signed up for the Legend of Zelda giveaway had previously signed up on my mailing list.

This is not common. Usually, I have 90-95% new subscribers to my giveaways, but in this case, I was only getting 35% new subscribers. I knew something was wrong, so I went digging. The advantage of experience is that when something goes wrong, you can almost always suss it out and fix it quickly.

First, I checked the cost per click (CPC). In this case, the ads were performing manageably but not optimally. However, they were being shown to existing subscribers instead of new fans. It was a big problem I needed to fix.

Facebook lets you exclude existing emails from your ad targeting, so I assumed that I had either forgotten to do that this time or not updated my existing subscriber information for a long time. So, I downloaded a list of all my subscribers and uploaded it to a new custom audience. In doing so, I decided to check the targeting also in the ad set level.

That's when I found it.

My ads were still being targeted at *Supernatural* fans. I had just spent half a day marketing a *Legend of Zelda* giveaway to *Supernatural* fans.

Doh!

That was a rookie mistake and one I only made because it had been over a month since I ran any ads. That is why I test, though, to find any issues with my ads, even if those issues are my own idiocy.

After beating myself up for a few minutes, I made the changes and started the ad set again. The next morning, I looked at my ad costs, hoping they went down.

The result? The next day, with the right targeting, I had a 50% cost reduction.

The difference of one CPC does not really seem like that much of a difference when you're looking at a single click, but when you expand that out to hundreds of dollars, it's massive.

That's double the amount of traffic, all because I targeted the wrong audience with the wrong information. I know this is very technical, but it demonstrates something many creatives do in their business.

They target the wrong audience with the wrong information. There is nothing wrong with their product. The problem is in the targeting of their product. If they were talking to the right people, they would enthusiastically love what they were doing. However, they aren't, so they are being met with blank stares and dead eyes.

Yes, your product may be broken, but equally, and often more, likely is that your product is fine, but your marketing is broken. Luckily, this was a cheap lesson for me to learn, but most creatives spend their whole careers talking to the wrong audience about a great product.

Either that, or they are going around asking people to follow them and making themselves the center of the universe. That's honestly the worst possible thing you can do both for your **own** mental health and your business **as a whole**.

Even if you are the center of your brand, nobody is buying anything because of you. **They are buying things because of how you make them feel about themselves.**

This will feel cynical, but that goes for everyone. down to your parents and best friend. It's baked right down to the DNA.

I listened to the Happiness Lab this week and the guest was talking about how your "soulmate" is the one who connects to the right smells in your brain that make them pleasing to you.

You **never** sell yourself. If you talk about yourself, it's only to convince people you have enough authority to deliver on their transformation.

You sell the transformation. Not only is this better for your audience, but it eliminates taking rejection personally.

Because rejection is not personal.

Rejection is saying, *"This transformation did not resonate with me right now"*, and/or, *"I'm not at a place in my life to deal with that transformation at the moment."*

Not only will it get you more sales, but it will also feel less gross because you are being of service to people.

Write for yourself, but edit for the transformation. Every story I've ever read that resonated in any way found a way to connect their inner journey with the inner journey of others in a way that sparked a transformation in them.

The #1 note I hear agents give to memoirists is, *"Can we make this more universal?"* which really means, *"How can we sell the transformation better?"*

It is easily the #1 note I give to writers who publish with us.

If you are having trouble growing your publication, I can almost guarantee it's because you don't sell the transformation well enough either in your work or the marketing around it.

Virality has nothing to do with you. It has everything to do with how you make somebody feel about themselves.

Always. Sell. The. Transformation.

All these very technical pieces become much easier when you have a brand. Everyone rolls their eyes at the word "building a brand", but I think they have it all wrong. They don't want to become a marketing machine.

A brand is not a thing you become. It is an expression of what you already are, expressed in a way that helps people who resonate with your work find you. Done well, a brand is something that speaks for you when you can't speak for yourself and calls out through the darkness to people who need to hear your message that you are there to help them.

You cannot be a light in the darkness if nobody can see the light or know that it is a friendly light and not a malicious one.

If anything, good branding helps you better inhabit the unique expression of your voice, not dull it.

It doesn't matter if somebody wants to make money with their work. I've never met an author who didn't want to find more people who resonated with their message.

You probably don't hate advertising. You hate seeing advertising for things you don't want. You probably don't hate marketing. You hate marketing for things that don't resonate with you.

You probably don't hate sales. You hate being sold things you don't want.

You likely love finding a new cool thing you really want that resonates with you. People can sell that to you all day.

The problem is you expect people not to want your work, that it won't resonate with them, and that they will hate you because of it.

What if, instead, they…didn't hate it? What if, instead, they loved it? What if, instead, they were grateful you showed them this thing they now love?

What if, instead, you stopped treating your work like it sucks for a change?

There is one thing I want you to remember in all this when things get hard. It's supposed to be hard.

That is not a flaw of the universe. It is a feature of it.

The universe makes it hard for a reason. I don't know what that reason is, and I don't think anybody else does, either. We can take a guess, but it's probably going to be wrong. We can study and philosophize about the why, but at best, it will only ever be an educated guess.

However, I have been on this earth for a few years now, and I've worked on enough projects to know that just because something is hard doesn't mean it's a design flaw.

In fact, more often than not, that thing people put into the game to stump you is integral to the design of the game. That level that you can't get through in a video game is that way for a reason, more often than not. That part of the book that's really difficult, well, that's to teach you something as well. Even lessons that we teach in school are often designed to be harder than they need to be, so students learn through struggling.

Sometimes, it's stupidly hard to the point of fatigue.

It's so stupidly hard that you fall off the cliff a thousand times trying to find a way off the island in the video game, but that makes the result all that more satisfying when you figure it out. It makes that growth even more pronounced.

Every time I've struggled in my life, I've come out stronger on the other side. With each struggle, there is also a chance for catastrophic failure as well. A player might walk away from the game or put down a book and never pick it back up again. However, usually, those failures gnaw at you until you get back and pick that controller up again.

I have found that it's the same in life. Smashing through the glass wall after hitting your head against it a thousand times is infinitely more satisfying than getting through the first time. Killing that boss at the end of the game is so much more satisfying if you fail a bunch of times, and it's way more satisfying than beating that first boss. Getting to the end of that series is all the sweeter when you've read the other books first.

Even if you buy every course you see and book every mentoring session with gurus. Even if you go to every show and have every connection in the world...it's still hard. All we can do is try to limit the pain, but we can't stop it completely. Maybe that's why it's supposed to be hard, to make it more satisfying when we get to the end game. I don't know. I do know, though, that it's supposed to be hard. That's just a feature of the system.

Trying is better than nothing.

Jumping is better than standing still. So many people say, "I'm gonna do it when X happens," as if there is ever a good time.

If there were a good time, everybody would do it. Even if you can only do something very slowly, you are 1,000 times further along than if you keep making excuses.

Starting gives you a baseline for growth. Once you have a baseline, you can progress from there. If you don't start, then you have nothing. When you don't start, everything is theoretical.

It's very hard to help somebody who's standing still. If you are moving, no matter how slowly, then it's so much easier to correct.

WHY I FELL BACK IN LOVE WITH ADVERTISING

As a person who specializes in author growth, especially the type of free or cheap viral growth that doesn't cost a lot of money, I have a confession to make.

I'm tired. I'm tired of showing up on social media. I'm tired of constantly coordinating collaborations. I'm tired of spending all my time and energy thinking about how to get the next subscriber to fall in love with my publication. All of it takes up valuable energy that I could spend on writing or recovering.

Which is why I fell back in love with advertising in 2023.

Cards on the table: I've always run ads for other people, but last year, I fell back in love with spending money on advertising for myself...and since I did, I've seen my subscriber number go up every single day.

It's not that I didn't get a lot out of our advertising when I did it. I just started producing upwards of a book a month and didn't have the funds to advertise and produce at the same time, so I chose to spend my time creating my work and launching it to my audience.

Since 2019, most of my time has been spent on producing and launching books, which has made me a lot of money, but my audience hasn't grown very much since then. I had about 20,000 people on my list back there, and I have 22,000 on it now.

I've had a great career and am not complaining, but to get to the next level, I at least need to double my free subscribers. The top, elite-level publishing experts/companies have between 50-100k+ on their email list, and I want to get there this year.

Unfortunately, with my chronic illnesses, I can't be present as much as I need to move the needle with social media. So, I have a pretty aggressive advertising plan.

Not everyone will be able to be as aggressive as me, but I think advertising should be a part of every writer's arsenal. Nobody talks about advertising as a way to build a Substack publication, but since I started spending $25/day on advertising on December 1st, my audience growth has stabilized significantly.

I started focusing on it in the summer of 2023, on and off until December, when I went hard on advertising.

I spent most of the summer testing various ad networks to see if any of them were viable for Substack audience growth, and here are my findings:

- **Refind**—Of all the ad platforms, this is the easiest to use. You basically give it a one-sentence description and how much you want to spend, and then it finds you that number of new subscribers every day. This seems to be most effective for people looking for readers/free subscribers and not members. I spent about $20/day for a couple of months, and it definitely worked for me.

- **Sample.ai**—I was excited about another choice outside of Refind, but I had to pay close to $5 per subscriber, and then I was only getting 1 a week. This is not a platform for value or quick growth. They do have a free option, which is worth trying out.
- **Beehiiv**—I've been looking into the Beehiiv ad network for months, and in August, they had a deal where they would match your budget up to $2,500, so I dropped $2,500 into my account and proceeded to hate my life for the next three weeks. Unless you are working in AI or NFTs, I saw nothing relevant to use to promote myself on their platform. Also, while they said you could find subscribers for $2, I didn't find any success until I spent $4, and that is way too much for me to spend to find a subscriber. I ended up canceling my account and getting a refund. At least I made $131 during my time to pay for the month I used it.
- **Facebook Ads**—I've been running Facebook ads for years and have always found them effective. I can find subscribers for $.50-$1, but in recent months, the subscribers have been riddled with bots, so I've mostly stopped Facebook ads except for clients with good bot filters.
- **Sponsoring newsletters**—We've been doing this through Booksweeps and Written Word Media for our Action Fantasy Book Club and have gotten consistent results. They charge between $1-$1.25 per subscriber, which is about what I get from Facebook after scrubbing, with none of the hassle. Currently, they both only do fiction, but sites like Who Sponsors Stuff, Reletter, and Paved have options for most niches. I haven't used those three, though. I also started using Voracious Readers Only , which sends me about 30-50 new subscribers

every month for $30. Since I started, I've gotten over 200 new subscribers to my fiction. I paid way more than that for social media management solutions before, with zero results.

- **Sparkloop**—I started using the Sparkloop/Convertkit paid recommendation engine early in 2024, and it's pretty great. I also set up an automation sequence where I broke up my hero post across these few emails and then followed it up with a pitch to my paid membership. I thought it would take a long time to get this set up like it did on Beehiiv, but because they allow you to "automatically accept pre-approved advertisers", I started getting emails for $1.25 each almost immediately, and it's been growing. I recently dropped that down to $1.10, and it's still working. One thing I really like about Sparkloop is that you only pay for people who have opened at least one email since they joined your list and didn't unsubscribe. So, you don't pay for a bunch of dead weight, which I've never even heard of as an option before from an advertiser. Since they charge you a flat fee a month, I guess they are incentivized to make it the best experience possible. The only negative of Sparkloop is that you must commit to at least a $2,000/mo ad budget to use it. You might not spend it all, but you have to commit to it. Still, I recommend it for now. I also like that if you have Convertkit, you can combine paid and free recommendations through their creator network, which is what I wish I could do on Substack, but I can't.

The best quality of subscribers comes from the Substack Network and Recommendations, but if you want to explode your growth, maybe you can find something you like above without having ads overtake your life. Overall, I think most of these efforts have been a bust, but they have led to engaged subscribers, even if they don't upgrade. I've been able to scale up from 16,000 to 19,000 while maintaining my open rates, which is nice.

The most interesting thing I learned came from Beehiiv, who told me they target spending $4/lead for their high-end advertising client, which is just bonkers to me. I still think that for most people, using viral builders is a great way to scale at a low cost, as long as you have a good onboarding sequence and are willing to cull unopens liberally.

Since I started going all-in on advertising late last year, my free subscriber line has smoothed out. Before then, it was a jagged mess. Now, it's going up (*relatively*) smoothly. Currently, I run advertising leads through a 14-day automated sequence before adding them to my publication. The time I spent setting that up, and thus not importing paid leads, was the first time since I started ads that I didn't see significant linear growth.

Most people I talk to don't want to invest in advertising and don't want to do social media, but they still want to grow their publications.

I get it. I want to grow infinitely without paying a dollar for it or investing any time, too. Unfortunately, if you don't want to be on social media, you can start doing paid ads and get the same effect or hire somebody to do it for you.

I go through this same conversation with most of my clients when we get started.

You'll be investing either money, time, or both. You can't get through that. No, there's not somebody who will work on performance for a person that isn't proven.

You either have to pay somebody to do it, pay an algorithm to do it, or do it yourself. The less you want to do, the more you have to pay.

The goal is to make enough to pay for the advertising/help and make a profit. Meanwhile, you get to do the things you like more, and hopefully, you will be able to be more productive so you can make even more.

I wish the world worked differently, but you either have to pay capitalism in time or money.

Right now, I use Refind, Sparkloop, Convertkit, and Facebook ads and spend around $100/day on them.

My problem with advertising in the past is that I had to watch it carefully every day, but I decided last November that if I used a system like Refind, I could set a price I'm comfortable paying, start an ad, and forget it.

In the same way, you can set a bid cap on Facebook ads and let them run, but they don't always behave. While Facebook is a lot harder to control than Refind, I also started sponsoring emails with the Action Fantasy Book Club last year, paying between $1-$1.25 per new subscriber.

Refind doesn't work for fiction, but sites like Written Word Media and Booksweeps offer that same sort of growth mechanic where you can set it and forget it.

Then, all you have to do is take those subscribers and add them to your mailing list. Yes, the quality varies wildly when you're talking about those types of builders, which is why I like sponsorships because they have to make an active choice to join your list.

If you have a highly engaging automation sequence, then you should be able to turn that into money…but even if you don't, what if you could stop doing the draining bits? How much would that be worth to you?

I decided that it was worth $25/day not to have to do any of it. For that, I was pretty much guaranteed somewhere between 15-30 new subscribers. If I pay to sponsor a Booksweeps promo, or even if I pay $60-$200 to participate in one, then I get those emails once it's done…and I don't have to do the marketing stuff I don't love.

I'm not saying you should pay $25/day for advertising, but even getting 1 new subscriber through advertising could stabilize your writing business. If you spend $1/day, that's between $28-$31/mo.

How much time are you spending right now on audience growth? How much are you growing a month? Is it worth investing in advertising to get a little bit of consistent growth?

For me, the answer was an emphatic yes.

Organic growth is great, but you need a core group of readers to start talking about your work before that starts to self-generate. I hear so many writers who tell me they can't get traction, and I tell them, "Did you know you can just pay for it?"

Yes, it's expensive. I've been paying for mailing list subscribers since 2015. Sometimes, I paid for them by buying a table at a show and collecting emails there. Sometimes, I did it through viral builders or group promotions through Bookfunnel, StoryOrigin, Booksweeps,

Litring, Written Word Media, and more. Sometimes, I ran advertising to free opt-ins.

I got away from it in the past couple of years, but I built my whole business through that kind of work, and I'm watching it work again. Now, I wonder how much momentum I lost, giving up on it for so long.

In 2024, I'm looking to get better leverage in my business, which means only doing the type of marketing work that I love doing and automating everything else.

Some of that means automating systems, integrating AI in ways that make sense, and hiring VAs, but advertising is basically automating audience growth, so you don't have to be there doing it all the time.

I've not seen great conversion yet into paid, but there is value in simply having a large audience listening to you every week, even if they're not buying. Marketing is all about lowering the cost of your sales efforts and finding ways to scale. Also, I've only had a paid newsletter for one year. Before then, it was all about gathering people who would buy other things, so I don't mind that bit.

In a perfect world, you would have a self-liquidating offer (SLO) that allows you to recoup most or all of your advertising costs. Sometimes, it's called a pocket course or any number of things, but the idea is that it lets you claw back the cost of your advertising.

They are a pain to set up, but they let you scale advertising much higher than you ever could without one.

You don't need one, though, if you don't want that burden. Just pick a number you're willing to invest in your business and start there.

In my younger years, I was most interested in monetization. In recent years, however, I've grown more interested in scaling my audience so that the highest number of people can hear my message. I probably would not be as interested in sources like Refind or Sparkloop if I were most interested in monetization overgrowth, but in this phase of my life, that is what's most important to me, so it changes how I view traffic sources.

I know we don't think about ads as automating audience growth, but after putting aside a budget every day and knowing I was going to spend that win, lose, or draw as my "penalty" for not doing social media, my life got a whole lot easier.

Writers simultaneously want to write what they want, complain about burning out, and abhor advertising…

…but advertising helps you build an audience…

…which creates leverage so you can make more money doing less work…

…which will help your burnout. I'm not even talking about sales advertising. I'm talking about using it specifically for audience building.

I have now had this conversation with hundreds of writers, and no matter what I say, they tell me advertising will never work or that they still hate it for some reason…

…then they still complain that they work too hard…

…for too little money…

…and that nobody appreciates their work…

…as if the magic audience fairy is going to bless them.

Here's a little secret.

Advertising democratizes audience business. It allows people who aren't blessed by the audience fairy to go viral and build an audience for their work.

Yes, it costs money, but it *literally* allows you to buy virality. I have been scaling up advertising for the past several months, and watching the audience numbers go up is wild.

Every time I see this happen, I think it's magic.

If you are not blessed by the magic audience fairy, you can just pay for it. No, it's not easy to pay, but every time I have stagnated, spending on advertising lit a fire under my growth.

If you are tired, fed up, burned out, and want to get more from doing less, you can exchange money for advertising, and it is kind of like buying magic.

PLANNED SERENDIPITY

I always thought that the more successful you became in business, the more rational, logical, and measured you would be, but I've had a different journey. I started in business very "business-minded".

I put quotes around business-minded because while there is a perception of what being business-minded means, my journey has been a descent into chaos. Traditionally, being business-minded entails possessing a mindset focused on business-related activities, including entrepreneurship, management, finance, and strategic planning. Individuals with this mindset demonstrate strategic thinking, analyzing situations to identify opportunities and developing plans to achieve business goals while also being willing to take calculated risks.

That's not to say my successful friends don't have all those qualities. They do. It just paints a picture of a stodgy old man who sits around a computer studying spreadsheets.

Basically, it brings to mind President Business. Meanwhile, most of my successful friends are closer to Princess Unikitty.

Let me be clear: ***Princess Unikitty is a killer business being***. They somehow keep Cloud Cuckoo Land running even though it is pure chaos, and they do it all with an upbeat smile and a heavy dose of magic. On top of that,

Cloud Cuckoo Land works effectively-ish, so much so that many master-builders choose to live there. In the chaos, they thrive.

When I first started in business, I thought it was Lawful Evil, like President Business, but I have found business is more Chaotic Good, like Princess Unikitty. Can you explain *why* Cloud Cuckoo Land works? No, but it certainly *does* work...until order is imposed on it.

To succeed, it's usually better for both your company and your mental health to focus chaos productively than to impose order onto it.

After that article, people asked me what they could even do if the world were pure chaos energy. I've been thinking about this a lot recently and I think my business started growing when I embraced that chaos and found ways to embrace it in more productive ways.

Mostly, I have fully embraced a concept I've been talking about called "*planned serendipity*".

It's not new. There are articles about it dating back over a decade. It's just new to me, and when I found it just fit a lot of disparate things I've been thinking about recently. There's even a whole book about it written in 2012. It wasn't very popular, but that doesn't make it any less powerful. As we often say at TAS, the popularity of a book has nothing to do with its quality. Let's bring Jeepers in again to talk about the generic business concepts we can take from planned serendipity.

Planned serendipity involves creating environments and processes that encourage unexpected discoveries and insights. Here are some main concepts it offers for putting planned serendipity to work in a business:

- **Diverse environments**—Encourage diverse perspectives and experiences within your team. This diversity can lead to different ways of thinking and increase the likelihood of serendipitous connections.
- **Cross-functional collaboration**—Foster collaboration across different departments or teams. This can help break down silos and encourage the exchange of ideas that may lead to unexpected insights.
- **Flexible workspaces**—Create flexible workspaces that allow for chance encounters and spontaneous interactions. This could include open office layouts, casual meeting spaces, or even virtual collaboration tools.
- **Encouraging curiosity**—Encourage a culture of curiosity where employees are encouraged to explore new ideas and interests. This can lead to unexpected discoveries and insights.
- **Serendipity triggers**—Identify and create "serendipity triggers" within your organization. These could be events, activities, or tools that are designed to spark unexpected connections or ideas.
- **Embracing failure**—Create a culture that embraces failure as a learning opportunity. This can help reduce the fear of taking risks and encourage experimentation, which can lead to serendipitous discoveries.
- **Learning from serendipity**—Encourage employees to reflect on and learn from serendipitous moments. This can help identify patterns or strategies that can be used to foster more serendipity in the future.

By incorporating these concepts into your business practices, you can create an environment that is conducive to serendipity and increase the likelihood of discovering new ideas and opportunities.

The main thing I take away from this is that while you can't force serendipity, you can bottle it. The more I embrace this business, the faster my success grows. My businesses are mostly about bringing the smartest people I know together, giving them space to exist as their best selves, and understanding that good things happen, even if I don't know what those things might be, effectively trying to bottle that chaotic good energy to work for everyone at scale.

The more I work building events, the more I believe events fail when they stop being able to bottle that energy for their attendees.

There is an idea in both publishing and movies where if you release enough books, then 1 in 10 books will pay for the other nine. Nobody can tell you which one will succeed, but they know if they release enough projects, then the Bell Curve will stabilize, and they can predict things.

That's a big, long way to explain that nobody knows what will work, but if we do enough of the right things, it will probably all work out. We all want more certainty than that, but I don't think it exists. *The best we can do is try to bottle chaos without imposing too much order on it.*

When I looked into it more, I found that this is true with almost any industry. It's how venture capital firms work. It's how mutual funds work. It's how innovation cycles work.

Basically, our entire economy runs on bottling chaos and planning for serendipity.

We as humans want to believe some people know what they are doing, but the "smartest" people are mostly just really good at bottling chaos and using it to get lucky. After all, *luck happens when opportunity meets preparation.*

You won't get your big break before your time. This is an unfortunate truth of being a creative. It doesn't matter who you know—until you are good enough to create mind-blowing content, nobody is going to hire you.

So many creatives believe that meeting Stan Lee or Steven Spielberg will change their lives. The thing is that it just might. It might change your life, but not until you are ready for it. If you meet Steven Spielberg and hand him your piece of garbage short film, he's not going to care.

If you meet Steven Spielberg with your earth-shattering movie, he might take notice. He might not, but he might if you catch him on the right day. But that meeting is luck. You have no control over luck. What you have control over is your preparation.

If you prepare properly, opportunities will present themselves. If you put yourself in the right situations, opportunities will happen. If you are prepared, you can make the most of those opportunities. The right opportunities can take years to cultivate, like pulling on a rubber band. As you pull back, the tension grows and grows. The harder you pull on the band, the more force it has when you finally release it.

The trick is to find these opportunities before you are prepared to utilize them and cultivate contacts until they will happily help to advance your career. This is possible even if you are at the beginning of your career and haven't created anything of import yet.

So, how do we do that?

There's an old saying among creatives: "Good, nice, and on time. You need two to succeed." Being good means you have the talent required to do the job. Being nice means people think you are generally pleasant and affable. Being on time means you deliver on or before a deadline.

As the saying goes, you need two to succeed. If you are nice and on time, you don't have to be that good. If you are good and nice, you don't have to be on time. If you are good and on time, you don't have to be that nice. It follows that if you want to find opportunities, you have to master two of those qualities.

At the beginning of your career, you aren't very good—at least not compared to where you will be in the future (with hard work and dedication, and finished projects). The only two things you have control over are being nice and on time. If you can master those two, opportunities will present themselves if you put yourself in the right situations.

If you can be nice and on time at first, even if you suck at your chosen profession, people will want to be around you. Over the years, you will build a massive Rolodex of influential people who want to work with you. Eventually, with enough practice, you will learn to be really good at your job, too.

Possessing all three of these skills is what I call the holy trinity of success, and it's critical to build your career. I've found it over and over in the top performers of every creative field. If you can start being on time and nice, people will want to help you. If you keep working at your craft, you will eventually get good. If you can be good, nice, and on time, there will be no stopping you.

It's important to note that when you get your opportunities by being nice and on time, these will be lower-end opportunities. They won't be hiring you for your dream career; they will be using you for grunt work.

If you can do that work with a smile, you will build up enough trust with people that they will assuredly want to help you at the opportune moment—but don't ask for that help until you are ready. When you can create great content, it will be a no-brainer for them to work with you.

It's easy for me to connect the dots of my career in retrospect, but most of it started with getting into the right rooms with the right people.

I recently wrote a comic with a very successful author, but that road started by reconnecting with her in 2022 at 20Books, and it really began in 2015, when we were both running similar companies. My relationship with our publisher goes back years as well, and we've both grown our careers in parallel but on dimilar (***different but similar***) tracks.

My partnership with Monica started in 2020, but it really started years before when I had her on my podcast.

I have maintained this idea for years that if I could know and hang out with enough smart people who were all on dimilar journeys, good things would happen. It wasn't until I merged it with ***intention*** and ***planned serendipity*** that it all started to come together.

The ***planning*** is the events and the spaces I either join or build with intention. The ***serendipity*** is what happens when you get there and let life unfold.

The more I focus on growing the right audience and curating the right events, the more my business grows, and the more I feel like I'm on a solid path.

I don't know what will happen from just about anything I do. I know that if I put certain projects out into the world, good things will come from them. It might sound terrifying, but it's one of the most freeing things I've ever found.

WHEN TO BURN IT ALL DOWN AND HOW TO RISE FROM THE ASHES

I made $50,000 more in 2023 than any other year in my whole career before then, and I nearly had a nervous breakdown trying to keep it all together.

I don't say that lightly.

I've dealt with depression, anxiety, and a myriad of chronic illnesses for years. While I am prone to hyperbolize, I don't ever joke about having a breakdown. The only thing that saved me was that I was so burnt out I became numb to how close I came to complete and utter collapse.

Fun start to an article, right? I'm not sure it gets more fun from here on out, but I sure do write a whole lot more words, so that's something, at least.

My Writer MBA business partner Monica Leonelle and I never set out to start a company together. In fact, when I licensed all my non-fiction work for her to use in her/our Book Sales Supercharged series, I never thought I would do non-fiction again.

I had worked in author service, book marketing, and courses for years by the end of 2020. While I loved the relationships I made during my time in author services, it was only part of my life that felt like a job. My clients consistently pulled my focus from writing fiction books, so after we closed the deal back in November 2020, I was excited to work exclusively on novels for a while.

It was an amazingly productive time in my life. I was writing close to a book a month during the pandemic and releasing 10(ish) books a year on Kickstarter. COVID was terrible for many reasons, but without doing 20-30 in-person events a year, my output soared.

Then, in October 2021, everything changed when Monica launched *Get Your Book Selling on Kickstarter* on Kickstarter, and the whole industry took notice. The campaign raised over $20,000 and laid the foundation for our legendary Kickstarter Accelerator course.

It changed again in March 2022 when Brandon Sanderson became the most successful project in Kickstarter history, making over $41 million.

Nobody expected that to happen, especially us. Suddenly, the entire indie publishing industry was clamoring for information on Kickstarter, and we happened to be in the right place at the right time to capitalize on that fervor with our book and Kickstarter Accelerator course.

When an opportunity presents itself, you have to act fast, so we pretty much put our lives on hold and launched the course by the time his campaign was over and interest was at its highest level.

The success we had with it completely changed my life.

However, we never set out to build a company. Both of us were successful authors with successful companies, and we both dropped an unplanned, fast-growth company into the middle of everything we were doing, and it quickly ate every moment of our lives.

What they don't tell you about fast growth success is that if you aren't ready for it, then it can destroy you.

Monica and I had never worked together before beyond that first Kickstarter, and now we were launching multiple courses, dealing with hundreds of students, and trying to keep our other companies running at the same time.

I was burned out by last September, while we still had two big launches and two more huge conferences to attend. I barely pulled myself over the finish line (and got COVID as a reward, the effects of which I'm still dealing with today).

By the time the dust finally settled, we had our most successful year ever...but it certainly didn't feel that way. It felt like we just worked harder than we had in our entire lives and had barely gotten anywhere.

In December, we basically decided not to talk for a month, enjoy the holidays, and regroup in January.

In the early days of the pandemic, I brought a proposal to a group I was working with to market our podcasts. The idea was to host a virtual podcast convention to build our email lists and build our reputation in the business podcast space.

I've run several virtual conferences in my life but never worked with so many people I barely knew. We spent about a month talking about it and planning it and finally reached the stage where people had to do a bit of homework to move forward.

I asked, and everybody agreed, to spend the next week writing 1-2 possible guests for each panel for us to discuss at the next meeting.

It wasn't a big ask, but it did let me evaluate if they were good candidates for partnerships. I learned long ago that before you go all-in on a partnership, you should set markers to assess whether your potential partners are likely to let you down.

I set this marker in secret. If people know about a boundary, then it influences their behavior. I needed to know how they would work when there was no pressure on them to deliver. It's really important to get a baseline assessment of the person to see if they are trustworthy or not.

I've consistently found that if a potential partner can't complete a simple task without supervision, there is no way they'll deliver in the clutch. I've carried too many group projects over the finish line to babysit business partners. On top of that, three of my own companies blew up in my face because I chose the wrong partners.

So, what happened?

Only one of them did the homework. So, I sent an email that said I was out because people didn't do the work.

They gave several excuses and even more reasons, but it didn't matter. Boundaries are important, and if somebody doesn't respect yours, you should find out early and get them out of your life.

This is how I go into everything. Small steps of trust with lots of ways to shut down because otherwise, you'll go too far down a road, and it never ends well.

The problems we had at Writer MBA were at least partially about boundaries, just not the same kind.

Monica and I had a different kind of boundary problem. Both of us were so used to running solo businesses that we dug in and did everything…even when it wasn't part of our ideal author ecosystem.

You see, Monica is a Grassland. She loves going deep on topics and writing about them from every angle. If you've ever seen *Hamilton*, Monica's answer to most things is to write her way out. She loves content marketingas long as she doesn't constantly have to be on camera to deliver it.

Monica needs silence to work in her zone of genius and huge chunks of empty space in her calendar. Meanwhile, in 2022, we recorded 80+ episodes of our podcast and were in constant launch mode.

As a Tundra, I'm more comfortable being on camera and recording live video because my superpower is excitement. However, I work best in short bursts with a lot of recovery time. My ideal schedule is a 2-4 week launch window with two months of recovery before the next launch, like a fashion designer.

When we sat down and talked it over, overstepping our boundaries was a huge reason for our collective burnout. Monica works best in evergreen content mode, working moderately and adding pennies to the bank, while I prefer working in heavy, short bursts.

Instead of working inside our ecosystems, we were trying to live in each other's, and it nearly destroyed us. Not to mention, we were trying to build a community like a Forest , optimize everything to peak efficiency like a Desert, and add different lines of business like an Aquatic.

It nearly destroyed us, and it took us half a year to even start to recover.

Even before last year, I have taken every December off since 2015 to do a complete audit of my business and reflect on the previous year. I plan new initiatives for the following year and scrap anything that doesn't serve me anymore.

If you've never done this before, then I highly recommend taking some time off to audit your career. Here's the exercise I do every year. It is a modification of the Eisenhower Matrix that is popular in productivity circles.

- Write down all your responsibilities and tasks, no matter how small, either on a notepad, a spreadsheet, or a whiteboard. Really, it doesn't matter where you write it down, but try to make it comprehensive.
- Create two new columns with headers NECESSITY and ENJOYMENT. The necessity column deals with how important a task is to the day-to-day functionality of your business. The enjoyment column deals with how much you like doing that task.
- Now, rank each of your tasks on a scale from 1-10. Something with high necessity can be monetary or functional, but not always. Some admin tasks are critical for a business, even if they don't add any revenue to your business. Meanwhile, some monetary tasks might not be very necessary at all. The enjoyment level should be self-explanatory. *Here's the rub.* You can't use the number seven as an answer. Seven is the default when you don't want to make a hard choice, so you can't use it here.

You must choose either a six or an eight, for reasons that will be clear very soon.

- Once you have your list, it's time to make a hard break between 1-6 and 8-10. ***This is why you can't use seven.*** Everything on the 1-6 side falls on the DON'T LOVE/DON'T NEED side of the barrier. Everything 8-10 falls on the LOVE/NEED side of the barrier, depending on the column.

- Draw a grid with four quadrants. Mark the X-AXIS as ENJOYMENT and the Y-AXIS as NECESSITY. Everything you LOVE and NEED should end up on the TOP RIGHT QUADRANT. Everything you NEED but don't LOVE should end up in the TOP LEFT QUADRANT. Everything you DON'T NEED and DON'T LOVE should be in the BOTTOM LEFT. Everything you LOVE but DON'T NEED should end up in the BOTTOM RIGHT.

- Now, you assess. ***What is in the top right quadrant?*** Those should be your core products and offerings. You might even find some new services you could offer that more align with your passions. ***What is in the bottom right quadrant?*** How can you make those more important to your business? ***What is in the top left quadrant?*** How can you outsource those or change them so you love them? ***What ended up in the bottom left quadrant?*** Cut those things ASAP.

What you should find are the things in your business that bring the highest return and provide a high level of satisfaction. You should immediately find ways to double down on those parts of your business. ***The more time you can spend doing those, the more your company will grow.***

If you find that you don't have any high-revenue products, then you should spend your time testing some quickly. When you're ready to move to the next step, you can do this exercise to help you plan your revenue for the next year.

No business can survive for long without best-selling products and/or services. If you've never done this before, it's going to be painful, and you are probably not going to like the result, which is okay.

When Monica and I met again after taking December off, we were still pretty fried, but we had a company to run, so we had to march forward into the future.

It would have been easy to continue business as usual, even if it would have killed us sooner than later. *That's what most people would do*, but the thought of that made me sick. I had finally made a life I was happy with, and being in constant launch mode just wasn't how we wanted to run our business.

If I wanted to be miserable in my life, I could just get a job.

So, we took a bold step, scrapped everything we built, and decided to rebuild our business from scratch with intention.

In designing our perfect company, we decided it had several components that allowed us to dig deep with our students. The first was a membership with an archetype system that created a framework for more of our students to achieve success quickly. That's where the Author Ecosystem fits into our plan.

The second was a conference where our people could all gather to talk about the future of publishing. This ended up morphing into the Future of Publishing Mastermind we launched earlier this year.

The third was a magazine to help direct the conversation. While we didn't have that third one in place yet, we were contributing editors to the October 2023 issue of Indie Author Magazine.

Mostly, we wanted highly skilled teams in place to help us grow while we focused on finding ways for our students to succeed. ***We couldn't do it alone anymore.*** It's literally taken all year to spin up all of these things, but after months of hard work, we're finally seeing the fruits of our labor.

We could have kept falling into the same cycle that burned us out in 2022. Instead, we chose to take a step back and find a way forward that worked better for both of us, respected our boundaries, and reinforced our ecosystems.

I've helped hundreds of authors in my career and watched countless creators become successful. ***The one thing that unites them all is that they have failed more than other people have even tried.***

They didn't get there overnight, but with consistent, focused, and intentional work, they figured out what worked for them and what didn't. One day, they seemed to lurch forward all at once.

It's like a jigsaw puzzle. You are given all the pieces in the box, but when you dump them out, it's a mess. Even though you are given a picture to look at, you only really learn how all the pieces fit by putting them together.

I watched them fail, and fail, and fail, and fail—but they never stopped. Each time they fell, they brushed themselves off, licked their wounds, and asked themselves these questions:

- What can I learn from this?
- What can I use next time?
- How can I make sure to never fail like this again?

It is that last word that is the most profound. *Again.*

They know they are going to fail, but they don't want to fail in the same way again. They learn from every failure, what not to do, and eventually build a toolkit for success, which they can use for the rest of their lives. Often, when I meet them, they are one or two pieces away from putting it all together—but that is where most people stop.

The successful ones don't stop.

They break through those barriers and end up successful in the end, not because they are more talented than other people but because they want it more.

Wanting it more doesn't mean working harder until you burn out. It means struggling against the barriers that prevent success, smashing through them using tools you develop, and learning from all the failures that pop up along the way. It means aggressively learning from everybody and everything around you so that you can soak up as much knowledge as possible and add things into your toolkit that might help you.

Notice I used the word might. Most things you try won't help you at all, but some will. You can't discount anything from anybody because that might be the thing that breaks you through. Some of my biggest successes were from studying companies like McDonald's and Starbucks. I was open to learning from them because I was willing to learn from anybody and anything, even though most things I tried were horrific failures.

Most authors fall into three categories with their ecosystems—unhealthy, healthy, and evolved. If you've ever heard Becca Syme talk about basements and balconies or listened to Claire Taylor explain enneagram growth, then this falls along the same general guidelines.

When ecosystems are unhealthy, they are performing actions that don't fall into their natural tendencies. A classic example would be a Forest trying to write to market even though they infuse too much of themselves into their books to have success working that way.

Meanwhile, writing to market is a perfect Desert strategy for success because they are great at analyzing the market and quickly writing books optimized to all the trends.

The first step in moving your ecosystem from unhealthy to healthy (after identifying your ecosystem) is to nurture the actions that give you a competitive advantage in the marketplace. If you've looked at the overview of each type, then you've seen that you can succeed in every ecosystem. However, a Grassland is going to have a nightmare of a time trying to launch like a Tundra because they want to spend years talking about and thinking about a single topic instead of launching well and moving on to the next thing.

This is the problem Monica and I identified above in our own business.

After you've identified the actions that lead to the best, most aligned results for you, then it's time to double down on them until you are not only healthy but thriving. Once you're healthy, then it's time to evolve.

Once you have a healthy ecosystem and you're rocking and rolling, it's natural to want to expand. We call that evolution.

For instance, my Substack is about going deep into the intersection of craft and commerce. That's a Grassland strategy I'm trying to bring into my Tundra ecosystem. I'm also expanding beyond books into card games, RPGs, and merch, moving into becoming a brand manager like an Aquatic.

If I tried to employ these strategies too early, they would have likely collapsed my ecosystem. In fact, I have tried to build memberships for years like a Forest, and they have been disastrous.

It turns out I wasn't expanding in a natural way for my ecosystem. As a Tundra, it makes complete sense to grow my brand like an Aquatic. I'm already great at curating experiences and launching, so it's a natural fit.

My love language is acts of service, so writing articles like this also works for me. If I can learn to focus on one topic, then I can grow like a Grassland as well. I've always done a lot of podcasts and content marketing during a launch. Now, I'm trying to take what I'm already doing and flatten it out to work over time instead of all at once.

This is equally powerful in building strong partnerships. Since developing this system, Monica and I have been better at growing our healthy ecosystems that amplify, not diminish, each other.

Even if I can't make content marketing work, that's not my success metric. I'm responsible for building out a launch, making everything connect, building excitement, and turning that into sales.

Monica and I have specialized in ways that reinforce our company's ecosystem, making us both stronger in the process. Now, we're looking for Forests, Deserts, and Aquatics to help fill out our team and make us even better.

One of the biggest reasons authors fail is because they try to evolve too quickly, while one of the biggest reasons that successful authors stall is because they don't evolve beyond their ecosystem. It's a delicate balance, but so is all of nature.

I left my last job (and hopefully the last job I will ever have) in June of 2015. That year, I made about $80,000, half from my old job and another half from being out on my own.

It was pretty evenly split between my only job and entrepreneurial pursuits. However, only about 25% of my company's money came from book sales. The other 75% of my revenue came from a Verizon dealership that I owned.

As a solopreneur, I made about the national average that first year. In 2016, I made about 50% more than in that first year. Of that, about 50% came from the Verizon dealership, down from 75% the previous year.

Since then, my business model has changed wildly with every passing year. My income doubled in 2017, but only 25% of my total sales came from that dealership. *The rest of the money came from selling books.*

In 2018, only 11% of my total income came from that Verizon dealership. Meanwhile, 56% came from book sales, while *a full 33% of my income came from book marketing and course sales,* two categories that didn't exist until that year.

My business has evolved and changed every year. In 2019, most of my income again came from book marketing clients, but in 2020, that income dropped by 85%, and my Verizon income dropped to zero during the pandemic. However, I made up for it by making over $70,000 on Kickstarter.

Last year, crowdfunding accounted for over $90,000 of my income, while my Verizon dealership never recovered from the pandemic. On top of that, I added a whole new company into the mix with Writer MBA, which changed everything yet again.

In 2022, I made $50,000 more than any other year of my life, and it was the first year I felt like I had figured out how my business worked, even though I nearly killed myself in the process.

Never again. I'm not about destroying my body to make more money. Monica and I proved our commitment to that by blowing up our whole company and building it again from scratch.

It seems to be working, too. ***This incarnation of my business life feels the best it's ever been***, and new opportunities keep presenting themselves every day. That wouldn't have happened if we had trapped ourselves in old paradigms that no longer served us.

I seem to have a knack for reinventing myself out of the ashes of my mistakes and adding new facets to my business that serve me better with every passing year. The more successful I've become, the more I reinvent myself to fit that success into my life. ***In fact, reinvention is the key to it all.***

If you're not happy with how things are going, you can reinvent yourself, too. It's never too late or too early. You're never too successful or unsuccessful to light it on fire and try something new.

HOW I "EVOLVED" BEYOND MY NATURAL AUTHOR ECOSYSTEM

I'm a natural Tundra. I'm a seasonal launcher who took to Kickstarter like a fish to water or a polar bear to hibernation. I'm a world-class hype man who knows how to build excitement around a launch, which has served me well for the last decade.

However, over time, I reached a cap on what I could do inside my natural ecosystem. This happens to most authors who have a healthy ecosystem. They find a natural limit to how much growth they can achieve by doing the same thing over and over again.

I could predict a launch down to the dollar, but I didn't grow substantially between 2017-2020. I was still a six-figure creative during all those years, but just barely.

On top of that, the landscape was constantly changing under me, and it became harder and harder to get people excited about every new project I had coming out. Even though I didn't know the word back then, it was time for my ecosystem to evolve beyond my Tundra instincts.

Evolving is the process of taking a healthy ecosystem and adding elements of the other ecosystems to help fuel growth. It should only be attempted once you have a stable ecosystem that is rocking and rolling predictably. One of the biggest causes that authors have an unhealthy ecosystem is that they try to evolve too soon.

I'm going to say it again because I know writers are stubborn. Evolution should only be attempted once your ecosystem is healthy and stable. Your ecosystem absolutely must run predictably without much variation because you need that stable income to fuel your growth, and you need the brain space available to take on new tasks that are outside of your comfort zone.

Almost all authors that fail at doing this end up evolving too quickly and destroying their ecosystem. This happened to me, as well, and I had to spend years rebuilding my processes after they collapsed. It wasn't until my ecosystem was stable and predictable that these strategies started to work for me.

If you evolve too soon, your existing ecosystem will devolve quickly, and you'll have to abandon your growth plans to nurse it back to health, wasting time and effort. Instead, first, focus on stabilizing and nurturing your ecosystem so that it can operate nearly independently from you.

Even though I know for a fact that many people reading this, even with my warnings, will think it's a good idea to evolve before they are ready, three warnings are all I have time for today. So, I'm going to move on and explain the strategies I used to build out my business beyond my ecosystem.

HOW I STABILIZED MY ECOSYSTEM SO I COULD EVOLVE LIKE A TUNDRA

Like many authors, I tried to evolve beyond my ecosystem before it was stable and success kept slipping out from under me. Whether it was writing to market, rapid releasing, expanding beyond books into other formats, building interconnected books, forming communities, or trying to "own a topic", none of them worked because every time I stepped out of the thing I was good at, everything I had built would crumble under me.

Now, I know the reason I failed is because I kept trying to move beyond my natural ecosystem before it was stable and predictable, but back then, I thought I was a failure.

Over time, I learned about the benefit of launching in seasons from JA Huss and Marc Jacobs, with quick bursts of live launching followed by long periods of recovery. This is the natural happy place for a Tundra.

I created a system where I would launch four main campaigns a year, with time to recover and rebuild my email list between them. Since I couldn't hype up Kickstarters for a full month for each campaign, I also started to cycle my campaigns at varying lengths, from 5 days up to 45 days, depending on the marketing demands and budgets of each campaign.

I eventually settled on doing a novel launch in January, a graphic novel/anthology launch in March, another novel series launch in June, and a comic book launch in September, with an experimental mini-launch in November for a small fandom-specific project.

Varying my campaigns and keeping to that schedule stabilized my income and allowed me to start thinking about expanding. It took a couple of years to stabilize, but by 2022, I was ready to expand from my Tundra roots and evolve into something new. Below is the order in which I evolved that worked for me, though every ecosystem has its own evolution path.

I can't stress enough that this worked for me because I am a Tundra. Building a healthy ecosystem will be different depending on your type. However, once my ecosystem stabilized, I was able to move on to evolving beyond my Tundra roots.

HOW I STARTED TO THINK LIKE A BRAND MANAGER AND EVOLVE LIKE AN AQUATIC

The biggest strength of an Aquatic ecosystem lies in their ability to develop systems to expand across different formats and involve different partners to grow their entire ecosystem. Unhealthy Aquatics expand too quickly before the scaffolding is in place, but a healthy Aquatic understands how to build their brand without collapsing under the weight of it.

This idea is naturally appealing to most ecosystems because they can rely on other people to help them build their brand. Unfortunately, for other ecosystems, the books drive everything else, including growth. For Aquatics, their growth is fueled by their entire brand, so they should be branching out into other formats well before everyone else.

Meanwhile, Tundras like me need to point back to successful books to be taken seriously by brand partners. I had been trying to put together brand deals for years, but it wasn't until I continuously focused on launch books that those successful launches started to bear fruit.

In the end, I didn't need to do much beyond showing my books were popular to open dialog with board game companies, coffee brands, and RPGs. Often, they came to me, even once I showed my brand had a critical mass of interest on a platform.

The growth of the game and publishing categories on Kickstarter certainly helped other companies take an interest in my brand, but only because I dug in deep on making my books popular on Kickstarter first, drumming up excitement, and using that to catapult my business into its evolution.

The key to my expansion was rooted directly in my Tundra ecosystem. The key to evolution isn't abandoning your ecosystem for another one. It's in using your natural state to fuel your expansion.

For me, the first successful expansion of my brand came from Monica incorporating my work into her Book Sales Supercharged series, specifically through the launch of *Get Your Book Selling on Kickstarter.*

Even though this was expansion through book licensing (more of a Desert strategy), it still showed me what was possible working with a successful business. Before I licensed my work to Monica, all the deals that I had been part of fell apart. Working with her was my first foray into expanding my brand beyond my own company that worked.

HOW I STARTED TO GO DEEPER WITH MY WORK AND EVOLVE LIKE A GRASSLAND

I started my career launching stand-alone books like the first volume of *Ichabod Jones: Monster Hunter, Katrina Hates the Dead,* and *My Father Didn't Kill Himself.*

Building excitement for a single book is one of the great skills of Tundras, and for the first years of my career, it worked really well. However, it eventually became apparent that the lack of depth in my catalog meant there was nothing to keep people coming back to read more about the universes they loved, which stifled my growth as an author.

While people do read cross-genre more than anyone gives them credit for, they don't do it enough to make a decent profit on a short fantasy series. For genres outside of romance and thriller, it generally takes four to five books before you can reasonably expect to make a profit on ads, which meant I had to write more books in the same series to fuel growth.

Since I didn't want to write in either of those genres, I decided that I needed to write a 10+ book signature series that could keep finding new fans for the rest of my career.

There is no doubt that this is a Grassland strategy as they are all about going deep on a few topics. However, I used my ability to gather excitement to launch not one but three signature series on Kickstarter (*Ichabod Jones: Monster Hunter, The Godsverse Chronicles,* and *The Obsidian Spindle Saga*). Instead of launching each book individually, I chose to launch multiple books with each campaign to garner more attention from my audience and direct the narrative.

While you can find Ichabod Jones: Monster Hunter on retailers, neither The Godsverse Chronicles nor The Obsidian Spindle Saga have even launched on retailers, yet I've already earned back all the money I spent on creating them and built a nest egg for marketing. When they do launch, I can use my skills as a Tundra to build excitement again to help that launch succeed far into the future.

HOW I STARTED TO INTERCONNECT ALL MY WORK AND EVOLVE LIKE A FOREST

As a Tundra, I've developed many more successful stand-alone books than most other ecosystems, but to have long-term reader growth, I needed to connect them all like a Forest.

To do this, I first needed to find my "shade trees". These are the books/series that stand out above all the others, attract readers into your ecosystem, and make them fall in love with your work.

Luckily, because of my work building three deep series like a Grassland (*Ichabod Jones: Monster Hunter, The Godsverse Chronicles,* and *The Obsidian Spindle Saga*), I had three different shade trees to attract readers. However, they were all pointing to different universes without much interplay between them. To get readers excited to read my whole back catalog, I needed to find a way to connect them.

I found that interconnectivity by creating The Cosmic Weave, a unifying concept I built around my books to connect my three biggest series with my standalone work to increase reader retention.

I've created the mechanics for nearly all my books to connect into one singular, satisfying experience for readers. It will take one more book to explain the concept, but once that capstone book launches, I'll have nearly everything interconnected for the rest of my career, building the bonds of my series like a Forest.

This interconnectivity is my attempt to evolve like a Forest, but it is fueled by my ability to build excitement and launch like a Tundra. Being able to launch a book successfully and break even on it allowed time for a lush Forest to grow with dozens of entry points that can drive audience growth for years.

HOW I STARTED TO FOLLOW THE TRENDS AND EVOLVE LIKE A DESERT

Of all the ecosystems, the one I struggle with the most is thinking like a Desert. Their superpower is finding attention arbitrage where demand far outstrips supply and delivering experiences readers gobble up with gusto.

This ability defined the career of pulp writers for generations, but I struggle with it. I have a deep-seated desire to embed my personality into everything I do and focus solely on the things that catch my interest, even if nobody else cares about them.

For Deserts, knowing the hot tropes and delivering a satisfying experience that audiences respond to is the goal, even if it means being invisible to the reader. Deserts make great ghostwriters, journalists, and licensed content writers because they can separate themselves from the work and be proud of whatever they are paid to write, even if they have no interest in it. They get excited to write a book optimized to hit as many hot trends or client requirements as possible, even if it means their voice is muted. Getting the story to pop with readers is the most important thing to Deserts, not infusing themselves into every page.

I envy that ability. I have no patience for or interest in optimization. I've gotten in my own way when it comes to money countless times for innumerable reasons. I've eschewed big genres with massive paydays because my artistic muse flitted to some obscure topic or another. I've turned away from life-changing offers because I didn't care much about the work. I even blew up successful companies because I didn't feel like doing it anymore, even if it meant disappointing lots of people.

My friend told me once, "What does it matter if you like it as long as people want to pay you for it?" and I scoffed at them while my bank account withered.

It literally took 40 years of my life for me to understand that when money comes easily, the rest of your life gets easier. So, I'm trying really hard to embrace my inner Desert more these days.

I don't talk about it much, but I've been burnt out on writing fiction for a long time. I haven't even started a fiction project in almost a year. Every time I do, I suffer debilitating panic attacks.

To help me get back on the horse, I'm working with my agent to identify genres I can write well that are highly saleable and don't take a lot of my emotional labor to finish. Hopefully, divesting the work from my emotional connection to it will allow me to move forward in a way I haven't been able to in a while.

Let me be clear: I care very deeply about doing a good job with all of this stuff. It's just that my whole essence isn't wrapped up in other people liking it or not, and that frees me to find even bigger and better hits.

I'm trying to be better about finding hits in top genres now. Even when I'm writing in my favorite genre of portal fantasy, I'm trying to think of ways to optimize my work to find the most readers. These days, I'm combining my Tundra ability to launch well with a Desert's natural instinct to find large pockets of fans and deliver a satisfying experience to them, amplifying both skills to take my career to a new level.

While everyone has an ecosystem where they feel the most comfortable, most successful authors will eventually reach a point where they must evolve beyond their natural state to achieve the success they crave.

This need to evolve also makes it difficult to analyze the ecosystems of very successful authors because they incorporate aspects of different ecosystems into their businesses.

Neil Gaiman is most likely a natural Forest. However, he found astronomical success with his long-running comic book Sandman and knows more about mythology than just about anyone on Earth, two traits that are pure Grassland.

He's also turned much of his work into other mediums, including movies and TV shows, which is an Aquatic trait.

It's very hard to be an uber-successful author without evolving beyond your natural ecosystem, but it's also critical that you know your natural ecosystem because when all the chips are down, you will revert to your natural state to regroup and regain your balance.

And what if you fail? I have started so many businesses that eventually failed, or I shuttered, that it's staggering. There's one thing about failure we don't talk about a lot.

The time you spend doing the thing you failed at has real, tangible value.

I recently shuttered my Verizon dealership after nearly 10 years. It used to account for as much as 80% of my revenue, but those days are long gone.

Those years where it carried my business have value. The relationships I made running it have value. The skills I built running that business have value. Most importantly, the money I made during that time had value.

People often only want to try new things when they are sure they'll be successful, but some things only serve you for a season.

That season, though, it might save your life. Additionally, the time you spend doing that task might have immense financial value in another season.

I stopped running book marketing in 2021 because it didn't serve me, but then a year later, an opportunity came up I couldn't deny that fit perfectly. Now, that one client makes me more money per month than my other sources combined.

Twenty years ago, I was a substitute teacher. I hadn't been in a classroom in over a decade, but last year, I brushed off the rust and started substitute teaching to get me through a rough patch. I have no shame about doing any type of work when things get rough or if I think it will serve me, even if it only lasts for a month.

Writer MBA sells courses and non-fiction books, but it's not my first time doing that work. In fact, I licensed all my work to Monica in 2020 because my previous attempts were miserable failures. I never thought I would do non-fiction again after that.

Look at me now. We've made more in the past year than I did in all my previous attempts at this combined. Those years I spent building those old businesses had value, even after I gave it up, and they helped me succeed years later. I made tens of thousands of dollars on those "failed" businesses before I shuttered them.

That Verizon dealership came from a partnership that blew up in my face, but I was left with the means to carry my business for years.

This also happens in fiction. My best-selling series was an abysmal failure when I first launched it, but retooling and relaunching it on Kickstarter brought new life to it. Now, that series is the lynchpin of my whole fiction business.

Somebody once told me that 99/100 businesses won't make it past 10 years, but 99/100 people make it past 40, which means people had rich lives before that business and after it. That resonates with me deeply.

Just because those businesses failed doesn't mean the years they spent running them didn't have value. They served their owner until they didn't, and that's okay. You can have a deep, meaningful life even if something fails. It can mean a lot to you, even if you decide to give it up.

It's not that failure is a life lesson. You get more out of failure than just a lesson. Sometimes, you get a lifeline. Other times, you plant the seed for success in the future. Most times, it gives you enough money to survive until the next thing.

Even if all you get is clarity on what you don't want to do with your life, that time has more value than we give it credit for, especially financially.

All three of my main sources of income are built upon the ashes of businesses that failed. Even before they failed, though, they served me…just for a season, not my whole life.

HOW CAN WE SURVIVE AND THRIVE IN THE NEW MEDIA LANDSCAPE?

People talking about the massive disruption happening in media right now are missing an important bit that we ignore at our peril, which is that large media companies exist, in essence, ***to work as curators of culture for their audience***.

They seem to have all forgotten this fact. Aside from massive overvaluation by venture capital, private equity, or opportunistic oligarchs, the throughline connecting every media company struggling right now is they have become terrible curators for their audience.

Whether it's a newspaper, magazine, publisher, TV station, record label, movie studio, etc., the thing they are doing, above anything else, is holding something up and saying, *"This is worth your attention"*.

They are sifting through millions and millions of data points to find the ones they think their audience will like the most. Sometimes, they find a hit, but even when they miss the mark, you can see their curation all over the things they choose.

The better you curate, the stronger your vision and the deeper the connection you build with your audience. A24 is a good example of a company that curates very strong vibes. You can tell an A24 movie a mile away. *I would die for A24 at this point; I love their taste so much*.

I used to feel the same way about Focus Features, but after NBCUniversal bought them, they diluted their brand until that strong hand of curation fell away. They are just starting to find that again. The same thing happened to Miramax, Searchlight, and many other businesses once they were acquired. *People came for the curation, and when that curation changed, their audience faded away.*

Great companies mold their brand to draw the right people in who will appreciate their curation and grow their audience through sharing those cultural touch points with more and more people. Fashion magazines are basically curation engines, from the stories to the covers to the advertising.

Over time, people learn to trust these companies more and more, because they share the same tastes. They resonate on the same frequency, and those things they curate hit the right bit of dopamine in their audience's brains.

Eventually, these companies create "mindless buyers". *This does not mean dumb buyers.* It means buyers who trust them so implicitly will buy without thinking because they trust the brand implicitly.

Good brands are only good brands as long as they continue being good curators for their audience. When they break that trust, people stop buying, or at least they start to think very seriously about what they are buying once again. Great companies are manically loyal to their audience. If Vogue started selling Sports Illustrated, it would be weird, and they would immediately lose their carefully built audience.

Media companies are cratering because:

1. They have grown beyond what their audience wants from them.
2. They have lost their way of curating what their audience wants from them.
3. They started valuing unlimited growth above being good curators for their audience.

We talk about how hard it is to grow an audience in the creator economy, but we gloss over the fact that *the real power in these, both new and old, media companies is in building trust through curation.*

Many people curate through their personality and writing, but others curate through creating roundups or lists or wish lists, etc., that others can search.

Good curation will never die because there's never enough time in the day. Curation is a beautiful gift for readers. A while ago, somebody told my Monica that when she posts something on her Substack, it means they need to pay attention. If she doesn't post, then they don't have to worry about it.

That is a heavy burden but also a beautiful gift.

No matter the platform, every creator is, in essence, standing up and saying, "I think you should pay attention to this". Those who "win" in the creator economy are actually winning the curation game. They create a symbiotic relationship wherein their fans tell them what they want to hear about, and they search out those things and make decisions on what they should pay attention to next.

It's a delicate balance. You have to give people what they want and what they need. It requires moving between the past, the present, and the future and laying them on top of each other.

In the new creator economy, curation is how we grow. It is how we know what to write, how to find other writers to work with, how to find cross-promotions to promote, how to decide where to advertise, how we choose how to build our platform, how to hire staff, how to strengthen the work we do, and how we deepen our audience's relationship to us.

People are not really subscribing because of your writing. They are subscribing because of *what* your writing can *do* for them and *for* what it does *to* them. They are paying for the time you have saved them in finding things worth reading. *People pay well for great curation.*

It is almost impossible to find somebody who can reliably give you information that feeds that dopamine hit in your brain in a way that resonates with you. *When you find one, you hold on tightly to it until either your tastes change or theirs do.*

This is why somebody like Gwyneth Paltrow can create something like Goop and succeed even though it was wildly different from anything they did before. She knew that the only game worth playing was becoming a curator of culture and developing trust enough in their audience that they would trust their taste.

That relationship is precious. It is everything in the new paradigm...but it was also everything in the old paradigm. Yes, the old media is dying in many ways, but in all the ways that matter, the game of curation will never die.

If you want to build a sustainable practice, the secret is curation. If you want to get more comfortable with getting paid for your work, the true value is in the taste you have developed and the time you've spent curating work for your audience.

We are all drug dealers, but the drugs we traffic in are serotonin, endorphins, and dopamine. We are all working to give that little hit in the back of people's brains that gets them to believe we are good curators of where they should spend their precious time and attention.

WHAT DO WE OWE TO EACH OTHER?

A few months ago, somebody asked why, given the negative reactions some people have, we should help anyway. I thought it would make a really good post, especially because it would let me dig into my deep love of philosophy in a way I don't normally get to do and do the type of deep research posts I haven't been able to find time for recently. If you want more of this type of thing, I recommend reading:

Why help other people? Let's start with the theoretical and philosophical. We help other people because we have a duty. Philosophy has multiple ways to view this question, but I think *The Good Place* frames the three main ones well: virtue ethics, utilitarianism, and deontology.

Let's start with **virtue ethics.** Created by Aristotle, virtue ethics posits that a virtuous or good person exhibits a collection of ideal character traits that present in specific ratios. Life, then, is about reducing and increasing those ratios to become truly virtuous.

What would an Aristotelian philosopher say about helping others? Probably, that part of living a virtuous life comes from honing virtuous habits like charity, gratitude, and kindness, and that living virtuously is the most, and only, noble pursuit. Thus, *we help other people because we want to be virtuous, and helping people is an intrinsically virtuous act that helps develop our character.*

But that's only one branch of philosophy. What do **utilitarians** or consequentialists say? Utilitarianism determines right or wrong by the outcomes of decisions. If you've ever heard "the ends justify the means," that was clearly utilitarian, the type who believes the most ethical choice is the one that brings the most good into the world.

They would probably say that the goal of a good life is to perform actions that result in the most good in the world and avoid performing actions that result in negativity in the world. Putting aside that you might be helping the next Hitler, *on the whole, helping people puts good out into the world and counteracts any bad you might put out into the world, especially if you do it selflessly.*

Finally, what would a **deontologist** say about this? Deontologists are the opposite of utilitarians because they judge an action as being good or bad, not the result of said action.

It shouldn't be hard to believe that a deontologist would consider helping a morally good action intrinsic to itself, and *we should help because we want to do as many morally good actions as possible.*

In all three main schools of ethics I've highlighted thus far, we help because the intrinsic good outweighs the bad, but I want to bring in **contractualism**, too, because it's not as much about what we owe to society as what we owe to each other.

Tim Scanlon wrote much about what we owe each other, and I highly recommend checking him out, even if I don't love the effective altruism movement that blossomed from his teachings. He argues that it's part of the social contract we all agree on when living in a society.

The idea is that we enter into a social contract by living in a society, and the things we owe each other are the things we can mutually agree on together. In that understanding, it's generally agreed that helping people is a moral imperative to lead a good life and foster a profitable society, so we should help because we want to create a better society for everyone.

There's a ton of work on this topic (it undergirds all of philosophy), but if you don't want to do all that work of reading, watch The Good Place, specifically seasons 3 and 4, which digs into this a lot.

In short, we should help people because we are a collective species that wins by winning together.

Now that we've talked about the philosophical, let's talk about the biological. One of the main reasons we have become the dominant species on the planet is from collective action and forming societies that interconnect us to each other.

Additionally, by helping other people, we allow them to specialize in ways we can't or won't. In building multiple businesses, I have found that most of it is shoring up your deficiencies with other people who do the things you aren't strong in to grow bigger.

Not only is it selfish to only help yourself, and it goes against the organic code that makes us up, but it's also a terrible business decision.

Every good thing in my career came from collaborators, ex-students, friends, fans, etc., helping me out. I've met all my best collaborators through giving and made hundreds of thousands of dollars from the "free help" I've given over the years. Not just from charging people for information, either. From co-writing books and consulting on projects and from selling lines of business to people that returned more than I ever made by myself.

When you help others grow, that growth is reflected back on you. If you level up your network, you level up too. Every good network pulls each other up when they get to the next network, and that allows you to introduce increasingly more lucrative behaviors with more successful collaborators.

There's no way you can collect all the lucky breaks, and by having other people out there watching your back, you give yourself even more chances to win.

So what do you do? You still help people, is my answer. I don't really care if other people hate me or like me. That's their karma.

What I put out into the universe is mine, and I choose to help people anyway, even if they don't appreciate it. Even if they hate it. Even if they scorn me for it.

Because some people don't, and there's enough of those people to more than make up for those that wish me ill.

Even if they didn't, I want this industry to be better and the world to be better, whether people appreciate me for it or not. I don't care about getting back what I put into something. I care about planting trees that will outlive me.

Life isn't a function of X inputs leading to Y outputs, and I would not care to live in it for very long if it was like that. Life is more interesting and complex than that, and doing this work is how I contribute my little bit.

PLG, SAAS, AND HOW THE NONSENSE TERMS FROM TECH CAN HELP SUPERCHARGE YOUR AUTHOR CAREER

I read a lot of tech articles, specifically about growth and scale, two words that are as exhausting as they are enthralling.

I am the first to admit that these articles are filled with nonsense terms and acronyms that make no sense. It's almost as if they have chosen the most complicated series of words on purpose to make sure laymen won't understand them.

Well, while I am not exactly a layman, I have spent my career translating business terms to creative people, and this might be my hardest challenge ever. Today, I'm going to take you through some of the terms that tech articles use, what they actually mean, and why they are important for writers to know.

By the end of this article, there's a good chance you'll tune out part way through because this stuff can be pretty boring, but if you make it to the end, you will hopefully be able to read these articles and understand what they are talking about, at least.

Ideally, you would understand how to use the strategies associated with these terms in your own business because while tech is a lot of things, one of them is profitable. They have figured out how to create seven, eight, nine, and up figure businesses online. So, they must know something we don't, right?

Well, hopefully soon, you'll know those things, too.

INBOUND MARKETING VS. OUTBOUND MARKETING

What it means: Inbound marketing is about creating content that people search for and that leads back to you. Outbound marketing is about you pushing your message to people through ads, calls, conventions, etc. If they come to you, then it's inbound marketing. If you go to them, it's outbound marketing.

Why it's important for writers: You need both of these strategies in your business. Inbound marketing usually takes a lot longer to spin up successfully, so you probably need to augment it with outbound advertising, at least at the beginning. In general, outbound marketing has a more immediate effect than inbound marketing, but inbound marketing can generate leads for a longer amount of time.

WOM—WORD-OF-MOUTH MARKETING

What it means: Customers share their positive experience with your product with other people. This can be organic, but you can also pay for this kind of advertising through influencer marketing or PR. Word of mouth is the gold standard. We all want it. It's usually the cheapest form of marketing but the hardest to predict.

Why it's important for writers: When we talk about readers talking about our books, this is WOM marketing, as is getting reviews, referrals, or many of the ways writers already want to market their work.

TAM/SAM/SOM—TOTAL ADDRESSABLE MARKET/SERVICEABLE AVAILABLE MARKET/SERVICEABLE OBTAINABLE MARKET

What it means: The complete market for your product is the TAM. This includes everyone, even if you can't reasonably work with them. The SAM is the portion of a market that you could work with inside the total market that you could theoretically work with. The SOM is the portion of that market that is reasonably attainable.

Why it's important for writers: Writers love to think everyone will love their work, but while your work might have a huge TAM, your SOM will be much lower and possibly too low to expect to make a reasonable living from it. If you can move from TAM to SOM, then you can have a more realistic vision for your writing business.

LEADS

What it means: People who could potentially become customers in the future. These could be gathered through marketing, advertising, or even outbound sales calls to bring people into your pipeline.

Why it's important for writers: Writers are often singularly focused on turning leads into customers immediately, but most tech businesses know that it takes time to nurture leads and turn them into customers. This is where places like your mailing list are so important because they help foster customers by turning leads into buyers.

COST PER LEAD (CPL)

What it means: An average of how much it costs to bring somebody into your ecosystem, whether that is through ads, organic reach, or other forms of marketing.

Why it's important for writers: Lowering your CPL, or at least keeping it under whatever metrics you have spent, is a big factor in maintaining profitability.

SALES FUNNEL (AKA TOFU/MOFU/BOFU)

What it means: The process of capturing potential leads and turning them into buyers. This is often separated into TOFU, or Top Of FUnnel, MOFU, or Middle Of FUnnel, and BOFU, or Bottom Of FUnnel.

Why it's important for writers: Writers often have no strategy for turning leads into buyers or understanding how they make sales. They know that if they turn on ads, money comes, and maybe those ads are profitable, but a sales funnel is the first step in understanding how to build a process into your business that converts leads into buyers.

PIPELINE

What it means: A visual way to represent potential buyers through the different stages of the purchasing process. This is the tactical process you use to draw people through your sales funnel.

Why it's important for writers: I often talk about the sales funnel as a way to bring leads into your business and turn them into buyers, but a pipeline is the strategy you use to do that. Every part of your pipeline is a different touchpoint that helps turn your potential buyer into a customer.

FLYWHEEL

What it means: While a sales funnel is a process of turning leads into customers, the process of a sales funnel is very transactional and basically ends when somebody purchases. A flywheel, in contrast, centers the customer experience throughout the sales cycle and creates a holistic experience that continues long before and after a sale.

Why it's important for writers: Writers are often great at creating a good experience for their potential customers, but they are…less good at asking for a sale, which is an integral part of owning a business. The flywheel centers the customer while also leaving room for sales as part of the customer experience. Personally, I think writers need to start with a funnel and turn it into a flywheel. If you know about our Author Ecosystems, we often say a Tundra is a funnel without a flywheel, while a Forest and Grassland are flywheels without a funnel.

SALES CHANNEL

What it means: A platform or market a business uses to sell its products. This can include places like Facebook, Google, or Amazon, but it can also include conventions, billboards, or outbound sales calls.

Why it's important for writers: Writers are not very good at looking at their business across sales channels or finding new sales channels to bring into the business. In the world of direct sales, we must be able to pull leads from different channels to succeed.

VALUE LADDER

What it means: A range of products and services at different price points intended to attract different types of buyers.

Why it's important for writers: Writers are very good at thinking in books, but books are only one price point, and even within them, you can offer ebooks, print books, hardcovers, special editions, annotated books, and much more at different price points to attract various readers. You can also include things like an in-person conference, VIP calls, personalized letters, writing people into books, and many other types of rewards to people to expand your business and bring in more revenue. This value ladder can be seen most starkly in the reward tiers on Kickstarter.

CONTINUITY

What it means: In a subscription-based business, the continuity is the money that you make every month. People also talk about this as MRR (Monthly Recurring Revenue) or ARR (Annual recurring revenue), which we will get to in a bit. On Substack, the Gross Annualized Revenue is the "continuity" of your business.

Why it's important for writers: Subscriptions are an essential pillar of any direct sales strategy. Even in the most successful businesses, continuity runs under everything to help add stability to a volatile market.

PROFIT MARGIN

What it means: When you take your overall revenue and subtract it from your operating costs, what remains is your profit margin. If you've ever had a job, you can think of revenue as your gross income and your profit margin as your net income once taxes and everything else are taken out of it.

Why it's important for writers: We all want to swim in a pool of gross, but we are trapped in a net of net. I heard Hector Elizondo say that in a movie once, and I've always remembered it. There are lots of "experts" who talk about making six figures a month on Amazon, but when you dig into it, they are spending six figures a month to get there, leaving them with very little profit at the end of the day.

CAC—CUSTOMER ACQUISITION COST

What it means: This translates to how much it costs to find a buyer for a product across marketing, advertising, and other outreach. Depending on the product, it can cost upwards of $150+ to find somebody to start a trial for a product. However, if that product has a cost of $1000+ and is mostly profit, then that cost can be easily absorbed by the organization.

Why it's important for writers: Just like tech companies, we are trying to find readers and turn them into customers. If we can better understand how much it costs to acquire a customer across sales channels, we can make better use of our marketing spend.

CHURN/ATTRITION

What it means: The amount of customers that leave your business during a given period. The average annual churn for a tech company is 5-7%, which means a company needs to grow by that percentage every year to stay stable. Otherwise, their income will decrease.

Why it's important for writers: Writers often tell me they are happy with the readers they have and don't want to do more marketing, but the truth is that even if you do everything perfectly, a certain percentage of people will stop reading you every year, even if only because they died. If you aren't constantly finding new readers, then eventually, you will have no readers left.

LCV—LIFETIME CUSTOMER VALUE

What it means: How much money a customer will spend inside your business before they leave your ecosystem.

Why it's important for writers: Every author wants to believe their readers will stay with them forever, but every business has a burn rate where customers will leave their ecosystem. Knowing the lifetime customer value of your readers allows you to plan marketing costs effectively. If you know that a reader coming into your ecosystem will spend an average of $50 with you, then theoretically, you can confidently spend up to $49 and remain profitable.

BURN RATE

What it means: How much cash you spend over a specific period.

Why it's important for writers: Making money doesn't matter if you don't have more cash on hand than you spend. Publishing is a war of attrition. You are often using this month's launch to pay for next month's launch and hoping to find your hit that will fund the next year of your business. One of the biggest reasons authors fail is because they run out of money before they find their hit. Knowing your burn rate allows you to judge how much longer you have before you run out of money.

RUNWAY

What it means: How long you have before you run out of money.

Why it's important for writers: As I mentioned above, a huge driver of authors giving up is because they ran out of money before they found their hit. If you know your runway, then you can work toward increasing it every day. I started with one month of runway, and we have built up a few years of runway over time. What you measure, you manage.

DAU/MAU—DAILY/MONTHLY ACTIVE USERS

What it means: A measure of how many people are using your product on a daily or monthly basis.

Why it's important for writers: While it's important to track sales, what really moves the needle over time is how many people actually read your work on a consistent basis. In this way, KU is a perfect measure of DAU/MAU. It shows not how many people downloaded your book but how many people are actually consuming it at any given time. The more people who read your work, the more people will commit to reading more. The longer they read, the more committed they will become.

YOY—YEAR-OVER-YEAR GROWTH

What it means: How much you have grown from one year to the next.

Why it's important for writers: Revenue is important, but growth is, in many ways, more important. If you aren't growing your author business, then you are stagnating and will soon see declines in your business if you don't do something to fix it.

KPI—KEY PERFORMANCE INDICATOR

What it means: Quantifiable indicators important to the success of your business. While there are hundreds of metrics one can look at to keep their business going, these are the ones a company is focused on to drive growth at any time.

Why it's important for writers: KPIs give you focus. What you measure, you manage, after all. While there are lots of things influencing your author business, there are probably 3 to 5 that account for the majority of your revenue. Maybe it's mailing list growth, TikTok views, or keeping your ad spend at a certain level. Whatever it is, if you choose a few that drive real growth, then double down on those, it will help keep you focused and allow you to give up on many things that don't serve you. KPIs can change throughout the year as well, but I recommend choosing ones you can focus on for at least a few months.

SAAS—SOFTWARE AS A SERVICE

What it means: Web-based software that customers pay for monthly to access their products.

Why it's important for writers: While SaaS is mostly about cloud-based computing, for our purposes, it's also about subscriptions. SaaS companies are trying to find new customers and keep them happy, so they continue their subscriptions. They're also offering different products to help increase the value of a customer over time. As writers, we should be learning from their strategies, even if the business they are running doesn't matter to us. SaaS companies are great at creating funnels and flywheels, and they have learned to do it at scale.

PLG—PRODUCT LED GROWTH

What it means: A business model where everything from growth to retention is led by the product. Companies like Dropbox and Slack, among others, are product-led growth companies where using the product, often through a free trial, hooks people into using it more.

Why it's important for writers: Does this sound like anyone you know? It should, because almost all writers are using this model. Books, publications, and anything where you are trying to get people to read your work as the main vehicle for growth is a PLG company. Free first-in-series, a trial membership, free book giveaways, etc., are all ways to hook people through products. PLG companies are wildly successful, with some of the highest profit margins in all of tech.

MRR/ARR—MONTHLY RECURRING REVENUE/ANNUAL RECURRING REVENUE

What it means: How much recurring money you make on a monthly/annual basis. This is really important for a subscription business like Substack because we make a lot of decisions based on the stability and growth of our revenue.

Why it's important for writers: Recurring revenue should be the goal of any successful business, as it gives us security in a chaotic world. It's the same reason we like working for a company. Stability is how we predict the future.

GRR/NRR—GROSS RETENTION RATE/NET RETENTION RATE

What it means: This is a metric measuring revenue growth over time. A good retention rate is 80%+, but a great company will be able to go over 100% by offering upsells. A gross retention rate measures all revenue, while net retention measures your revenue after expenses.

Why it's important for writers: I'm starting to sound like a broken record, but we want to be growing our business over time. This is another metric that can help us learn how our business is doing and how we are growing.

B2B VS. B2C VS. D2C—BUSINESS TO BUSINESS VS. BUSINESS TO CUSTOMER VS. DIRECT TO CUSTOMER

What it means: When you tease out what they mean, these three are pretty simple to understand. Business to Business means a business is selling to another business. Publishers have used a business-to-business model for generations. Their client is not the customer; it's the bookstores and libraries that stock their books. In general, indie authors run a business-to-customer business, which means selling to customers through a distributor like Amazon. The direct-to-customer model is what's coming now with direct sales, where we take ownership of the entire customer journey.

Why it's important for writers: The world is changing and we writers are taking more control of the sales journey to our customers. In doing so, we have to learn the difference between these three business models. Authors often want to sell to libraries, but they are not set up to do so because those have not historically been our customers. If we want to sell to certain customers, we must learn how those types of businesses work.

ICA—IDEAL CUSTOMER AVATAR

What it means: The customer who will cost the least to acquire (CAC) and spend the most in your business over time (LCV).

Why it's important for writers: Most authors try to appeal to everyone, but that is impossible. Instead, they should define their ideal customer avatar and try to find more of them. With eight billion people in the world, it's easier to find more excited people than trying to turn people who don't like your work to people who love it, which is unlikely ever to happen.

NPS—NET PROMOTER SCORE

What it means: How happy somebody is with your business and how likely they are to enthusiastically promote your work to other people. This is a metric usually conducted through surveys, and there are all sorts of these metrics. These are based on a Likert Scale. While a 10-point scale is the more common, you can use a 5-point or 7-point as well, among others.

Why it's important for writers: The most important thing to note about Likert Scales is that unless somebody is a 9 or a 10, they are not going to promote you to other people. If you're looking for evangelists for your brand, you should look to people who are in the 9-10 range. Additionally, these are the people you should be trying to find more of as often as possible. Develop your ideal customer avatar from these people.

ACTIVATION RATE

What it means: The percentage of people who take a desired action like making a sale, signing up for a mailing list, joining a promotion, etc..

Why it's important for writers: It's easy enough to understand why knowing how many people led to sales can be an important metric, but it's also important to know this when you join promotions and give away free books so you know which promotions to join, and which are ineffective.

TRIAL CONVERSION RATE

What it means: The number of people who started a trial membership continued once the trial membership was over.

Why it's important for writers: This metric is why I offer free trials for my publication. I figured that if it was good enough for big tech, it was good enough for me. I don't have a great trial conversion, but it turns out that 10% is pretty good. One reason to look at these metrics is to judge how successful you are and what you should be pegging as your success metric. Additionally, if you are giving away free books, you can use this metric to judge how many people convert to buyers for the rest of the series.

ACV—AVERAGE CART VALUE

What it means: The average dollar amount somebody spends when they check out from your sales platform. This could be Kickstarter or Patreon, but it will normally be either your web store or landing page.

Why it's important for writers: If you know how much somebody spends, then you can work on ways to increase that through cross-selling and upselling.

CROSS-SELLING VS. UPSELLING

What it means: Upselling means taking a base product and upgrading it with additional bits and bobs to make it more complete. Cross-selling means taking a product and adding other products to make it a more complete experience.

Why it's important for writers: If done right, 20% of buyers will purchase an upsell or cross-sell, so it's really important to add this to your business. Since these upsells and cross-sells are often between 2-10x the worth of your base product, it could double or triple your revenue.

LVR—LEAD VELOCITY RATE

What it means: How many leads you acquire and close in a given time.

Why it's important for writers: Having a ton of emails that don't convert into sales for eternity isn't very good for your business or mental state. We need to find ways to take those leads and turn them into money. One of the best ways to do that is to increase the speed by which a lead converts to a sale.

ASP—AVERAGE SALES PRICE

What it means: While ACV judges the revenue from your entire store, ASP deals with the average sales price of each item.

Why it's important for writers: In direct sales, some products are great as add-ons to increase cart value, but they are not very good on their own. This helps you suss out any stinkers and try to find ways to use them more effectively.

EOL—END OF LIFE

What it means: When a product stops being supported by sales, marketing, and support.

Why it's important for writers: We writers tend to think everything should sell forever, but the truth is that some things should probably not be supported or only be supported by bundles to retain your sanity. It's not so bad to have books up forever on Amazon or behind a paywall, but sometimes, a product on your direct sales store does more harm than good.

ARPU—AVERAGE REVENUE PER USER

What it means: How much you made from each subscriber during a given time.

Why it's important for writers: When you are trying to judge marketing spend, it's very important to know how much you can expect to make from them. It's often not very helpful to judge any single user, but taking a group of users, or even subscribers, to your mailing list becomes a good metric to judge how much effort to put into a marketing promotion. I find this really helpful for my mailing list, as I know how much I can expect to make from a promotion depending on how many emails I get, even if they came in during a free promotion.

IQL/MQL/SQL—INFORMATION QUALIFIED LEAD/MARKETING QUALIFIED LEAD/SALES QUALIFIED LEAD

What it means: An IQL is the weakest lead. They have just learned your company exists. An MQL is somebody who has seen some of your marketing and is interested in hearing more. An SQL is somebody who is ready for a deeper conversation. You can think of an IQL as somebody at the TOFU, an MQL as somebody at the MOFU, and an SQL as somebody at the BOFU.

Why it's important for writers: As we are building out a sales funnel, we need metrics to determine where a potential customer is in the decision-making process. These terms give us language to talk about how we measure our funnel and what we measure we manage.

PQL—PRODUCT QUALIFIED LEAD

What it means: Somebody who has experienced your product by some measure.

Why it's important for writers: These are the people who have downloaded and read something you have written. We like to think that everyone who downloads our book reads it, but in reality, only a small fraction will read our books after downloading, and we need to focus on how to get them to read our work.

CRO—CONVERSION RATE OPTIMIZATION

What it means: Increasing the number of people completing a desired action on your webpage. This could be signing up for a freebie, buying a book, or any number of things.

Why it's important for writers: We want more people to read our books, and we want to spend less money doing it. To do that, we must optimize our conversions.

CTR—CLICK-THROUGH RATE

What it means: The number of people who have clicked on a piece of marketing divided by the total number of people who have seen a piece of marketing.

Why it's important for writers: If we are running ads or doing any promotion, we want to know not only the total number of people who engaged with us but also how many people clicked and how many people saw it. Those optimizations can allow us to make the most of a limited budget.

USP—UNIQUE SELLING PROPOSITION

What it means: A positioning strategy that tells a customer how you are different from all the other competitors in your industry.

Why it's important for writers: While it's good to blend into certain tropes, it's also important to think about the unique things you bring to your audience. It might be that your books are really on-trend or that they twist a trope in an interesting way. Whatever it is, your unique selling proposition can help you stand out from the rest of the market.

UX/UI—USER EXPERIENCE/USER INTERFACE

What it means: The way users interact with a product. The UI is how the product is designed, and the UX is the user's interaction with it.

Why it's important for writers: If we care about readers at all, we should want to deliver a great product they will love, but the UX extends into every part of your business and every way a reader interacts with it.

MUV—MONTHLY UNIQUE VISITOR

What it means: How many people visit a webpage or website every month.

Why it's important for writers: Theoretically, if you can increase the monthly traffic to your website, you should rank better through SEO, get in front of more people, and have more people buy your product.

CPM—COST PER MILLE (THOUSAND)

What it means: The cost of showing your ads to a thousand people.

Why it's important for writers: You won't usually drive traffic using a CPM strategy, but sometimes it can be very helpful when ads are not performing well to see if maybe people are bidding on your search terms and driving up the costs, which you can see most clearly looking at CPM.

CONVERSION PATH

What it means: The process by which an anonymous human becomes a buyer.

Why it's important for writers: Most writers have no idea how to turn an anonymous user into a buyer, which is something that tech companies obsess over and have lots of data to share.

FRICTION

What it means: Anything that slows down or impedes a potential customer from taking a desired action.

Why it's important for writers: The one thing almost every writer has is a billion friction points in their business. It's like they intentionally want people not to buy their work. Then, they complain nobody buys their books. The easier you make it to buy your work, the more people will buy it.

PPC—PAY-PER-CLICK

What it means: This is a term used for a group of advertising options from Google to Facebook, where you pay when somebody clicks on a link instead of paying by how many people see a piece of advertising.

Why it's important for writers: At some point in your career, you will do PPC advertising, and tech companies probably do it better than anyone else.

CPC—COST PER CLICK

What it means: If you are using PPC advertising, CPC is the cost per click of that type of advertising.

Why it's important for writers: If you are using PPC advertising, you will be charged by the CPC.

CTA—CALL TO ACTION

What it means: A call-to-action is a button or link in a piece of marketing that gets somebody to take an action depending on the page offer. In general, you want one single call to action on a sales page.

Why it's important for writers: Writers need to get better at honing in on their call to action and providing 1 per piece of marketing instead of 10.

CAPITAL

What it means: The amount of money available to pay for day-to-day operations and growth.

Why it's important for writers: We need money to do business. Having enough money allows us to stay in business.

DELIVERABLE

What it means: The product that will be sent to customers or offered for sale.

Why it's important for writers: This is just a fancy way of saying product, and we all sell products, though tech companies say they "ship deliverables".

R&D—RESEARCH AND DEVELOPMENT

What it means: Research and development is the department that plans future products and services.

Why it's important for writers: Though we usually do it ourselves, we are always reading books and trying to figure out new trends in the market.

A/B TESTING

What it means: A/B testing, or split testing, means taking multiple options for something and testing them against each other. This often pops up when dealing with ads or landing pages, but it can be used for anything.

Why it's important for writers: If you've ever questioned any choice, you can use split testing to see the best path forward.

SEO—SEARCH ENGINE OPTIMIZATION

What it means: Improving your website so that you show up higher in search engine rankings.

Why it's important for writers: If you are a Grassland, then your success path relies on content marketing, which is the cornerstone of SEO. We all want to be found when people search for things, but if you are a Grassland, then this is mission-critical.

P&L—PROFIT AND LOSS

What it means: A report that outlines how much you made, how much you spent, and how much is left over for a given time.

Why it's important for writers: I can't ever say this enough. Getting your financial house in order allows you to write more freely.

ROI—RETURN ON INVESTMENT

What it means: How much money you have left after spending money on something.

Why it's important for writers: Anything that has a positive ROI is something you should probably double down on, as long as it doesn't take too much from you energetically or take you away from doing things you love.

COGS—COST OF GOODS SOLD

What it means: All of the costs related to the production and sale of products.

Why it's important for writers: One of the most important reasons to care about COGS is that in the USA, you cannot deduct the cost of goods (i.e., books) until you sell them. So, if you carry inventory from one year to the next, you cannot write off the cost of that inventory.

DATA ANALYTICS

What it means: Analytics programs allow people to identify insights born from measurable data. Companies like Google Analytics help people make business decisions by providing ways to analyze data.

Why it's important for writers: So much success in publishing is based upon analyzing data, whether it's researching trends, planning ad spend, or deciding what conventions to attend.

BI—BUSINESS INTELLIGENCE

What it means: Strategies and tactics used to analyze business information and transform it into actionable insights, usually combined with data analytics.

Why it's important for writers: When we analyze data to make decisions, we are performing BI.

BENCHMARKING

What it means: Benchmarking means setting clearly definable goals by which you will judge the success (or failure) of certain business objections and analyze the success of your business.

Why it's important for writers: By setting benchmarks before performing actions in our business, we can take some of the uncertainty out of an uncertain business.

MARKET PENETRATION/SATURATION

What it means: A measure of how much a product is being used by its target customers.

Why it's important for writers: We can use this metric to analyze how many books we've sold against how many more readers are in any market.

EBITA—EARNINGS BEFORE INTEREST, TAXES, AND AMORTIZATION

What it means: Frankly, this is a dumb metric used by unprofitable companies to show they are doing better than they are to investors.

Why it's important for writers: None. I only put this in here to tell you that if you hear about EBITA, you should assume the company is unprofitable and grasping at straws to prove to investors that they should give them money anyway.

RETARGETING

What it means: An advertising tactic to tailor ads to people who have gone to your website and not bought anything.

Why it's important for writers: Retargeting is the key to direct sales. If you aren't using retargeting and you have a direct sales offer, this can seriously increase your sales.

FINAL THOUGHTS

Tech industry terms are dumb, but as my wife so astutely pointed out, every industry has acronyms and specific terms. In all cases, they are dumb to outsiders.

I don't think tech terms are any dumber than any other terms in any industry, and they can actually be quite helpful to writers, especially those of us trying to grow through selling books and/or building a continuity program.

Tech is a great model because they are successful at doing the things we want to do, and they have been doing it for long enough that we can glean a lot from their success.

If we can peel off even a small sliver of their success, then we will be well on our way to building successful businesses. It can be frustrating, but once we unlock the terminology, the sky's the limit of what we can do with it.

WHAT'S NEXT?

It's over!

If you've read this far, I want to thank you for your persistence and perseverance. I know that learning about business isn't any creator's favorite thing to do in the world; however, just by reading this book, you are so much further ahead than most creatives on this planet.

I would say to give yourself a round of applause, but I've worked very hard throughout this book not to be cheesy and don't want to ruin it now.

Well, maybe just a little applause would be okay. Not too long, though, because now the real work begins.

That's right…work.

As much knowledge as I crammed into this book, it's truly just a primer to gear you up for a lifelong pursuit of learning about the business of art. The goal of this book is to give you the necessary tools so you can go out there and build the foundation of a creative career.

It's not an endpoint. It's a beginning.

You made it to the end of this book. Now, you are prepared for the horrible and yet consistent world of late-stage capitalism. However, you still have to live in it.

If you loved this book, I hope you go check out *The Author Stack,* my weekly newsletter that goes into even more depth about how to build your creator career.

https://www.theauthorstack.com/

As a paid member, you get access to a ton of my previous work, including fiction, non-fiction, courses, and more.

RESOURCES:

- *How to Build Your Creative Career*
- *How to Become a Successful Author*
- *Advanced Growth Tactics for Authors*
- *Get Your Book Selling on Kickstarter*
- *Get Your Book Selling on Facebook*
- *Get Your Book Selling with Cross-Promotion*
- Get Your Book Selling at Events and Signings
- *Get Your Book Selling in Print*
- *The Author Ecosystems*
- Create Profitable Facebook Ads course
- Fund Your Book with Kickstarter course
- How to set up and run an awesome anthology course
- How to run a viral giveaway to build your mailing list
- Write a Great Novel course
- How to Build an Audience from Scratch minicourse
- 10x your productivity course
- Lessons and lectures
- Interview archive
- Complete Creative data archive
- Income reports since 2018
- Script library

FICTION:

- *Dragon Strife* **(Entire five book series)**
- *The Void Calls Us Home*
- *The Vessel*
- *Sorry for Existing*
- *White Rabbit*

- *My Father Didn't Kill Himself*
- *Invasion*
- *The Marked Ones*
- *Anna and the Dark Place*
- *Worst Thing in the Universe*
- *Time is a Flat Circle*
- *Gumshoes: The Case of Madison's Father*
- *One Damned Good Thing*
- *Screw this Webcomic*
- *I'll Kill You*
- *Paradise*
- *Gherkin Boy and the Dollar of Destiny*
- *How NOT to Invade Earth*
- *Black Market Heroine*
- *Pixie Dust*
- *Katrina Hates the Dead*
- *Ichabod Jones: Monster Hunter*

There's probably even more now since I update it every couple of months.

You can also find my work at: www.russellnohelty.com

Feel free to email me at russell@wannabepress.com and let me know what you think, and please leave a review. The only way I know I should keep writing these kinds of books is from your reviews and kind words.

Find more of my work at my blog:

www.theauthorstack.com

Find all my work at my website:

www.russellnohelty.com

Bookbub:

https://www.bookbub.com/profile/russell-nohelty